To, Nat & N'
you guys ..... mother
to our girls! We love ya'll!
♡ Margaret & Neil
4/22

Another Mother

Praise for *Another Mother*

"If all photos are ultimately about the photographer as much as the subject, *Another Mother* operates under a similar rule, with earnest, heartwarming results, carried along by stylish writing. By learning so much about Dezna we learn perhaps even more about Urken, which only serves to reinforce the main theme of the book: As different as the nanny and her charge's lives and experiences were from each other, they were and still are inseparable."

—The Los Angeles Review of Books

"Urken's *Another Mother* is a rollicking romp across Jamaica and his past that pulls at the heart strings. Written in muscular prose, the memoir is at once an adventure quest and an emotional reckoning."

—Newsweek

"Urken's resonant debut memoir doubles as a biographical tribute to Dezna Sanderson, the 'Jamaican Mary Poppins' who helped raise him for over a decade...A memorable hybrid of heartfelt memoir and fond commemoration framed in Caribbean history, familial turmoil, and unconditional maternal love."

—Kirkus Reviews

"A moving and intimate portrait of a remarkable woman, this book gives definitive proof that mothering need not come from one's mother, that one can learn stability and generosity elsewhere. The book is nostalgic and moving, the bildungsroman of a man determined to understand the life of the woman who in so many ways gave him his own."

—Andrew Solomon, author of *The Noonday Demon*

"A brilliant meditation on the complexities of family, identity, immigration and, ultimately, love. A story as rich in unique cultural dynamics as it is resonant with universal themes: who are the people we call our family, what hurts and hopes do we hide from each other, and to what lengths are we willing to go truly to know the ones we love?"

—Taiye Selasi, author of *Ghana Must Go*

"The Jamaican women who left the country in the 1970s and 1980s took on unthinkable challenges to provide for their families back in Yard. Many, of course, worked as nannies in the US, a history that is well-known but little explored. In *Another Mother*, Ross Kenneth Urken poetically unpacks the legacy his nanny, Dezna Sanderson, left on his life and examines how her immigration ultimately linked two families – his and hers – in a beautiful, modern twist."

—Andrew Holness, Prime Minister of Jamaica

"[A] relentless search for purposefulness amid the din of daily living. Authentic and deftly written."

—Jamaica Gleaner

"A 'perfect' book has a number of entry points…Urken's wry sense of humour, perfectly timed anecdotes and crisp, concise personal history along with snippets of Jamaican history make this a finely nuanced memoir."

—Trinidad and Tobago Newsday

Another Mother

A Jamaican Woman, The Jewish Boy She Raised and His Quest for Her Secret History

Ross Kenneth Urken

IAN RANDLE PUBLISHERS
Kingston • Miami

First published in Jamaica, 2019 by
Ian Randle Publishers
16 Herb McKenley Drive
Box 686
Kingston 6
www.ianrandlepublishers.com

© 2019 Ross Kenneth Urken
    978-976-8286-06-2 (pbk)

National Library of Jamaica Cataloguing-In-Publication Data

Names: Urken, Ross Kenneth, author.
Title: Another mother : a Jamaican woman, the Jewish boy she raised and his quest for her secret history / Ross Kenneth Urken.
Description: Kingston : Ian Randle Publishers, 2019.
Identifiers: ISBN 9789768286062 (pbk).
Subjects: LCSH: Sanderson, Dezna, 1941-2010. | Child care workers – United
    States. | Child care workers – Jamaica. | Nannies – United States. | Identity (Psychology) – Jamaican influences. |Jamaica – Social life and Customs.
Classification: DDC 920 -- dc 23.

All rights reserved. No part of this publication may be reproduced, stored in a retrieval system or transmitted in any form or by any means electronic, photocopying, recording or otherwise, without the prior permission of the publisher and author.

Illustration, Cover and Book Design by Ian Randle Publishers
Printed and Bound in the United States of America

For Dezna and Tiffan

"There are years that ask questions and years that answer."
— Zora Neale Hurston, Their Eyes Were Watching God

"Language most shows a man: Speak, that I may see thee."
— Ben Jonson, Timber or Discoveries Made Upon Men and Matter

Author's Note

This is a work of non-fiction. I have, however, taken certain storytelling liberties by adjusting the chronology of some events to streamline the narrative structure. In addition, though I did record and reproduce verbatim some conversations in this book, I have also relied on reconstructed and composite dialogue in particular scenes.

Contents

Chapter	1.	As It Was in the Beginning	1
Chapter	2.	Of Melodies Pure and True	19
Chapter	3.	Miss Dezna	29
Chapter	4.	Mum's the Word	38
Chapter	5.	Exodus	46
Chapter	6.	Thanks and Praise	61
Chapter	7.	Nanny of the Maroons	70
Chapter	8.	Could You Be Loved?	83
Chapter	9.	Fleeing the Nest	91
Chapter	10.	Jamrock-A-Bye	93
Chapter	11.	Mother of Invention	106
Chapter	12.	Blue-Blue	113
Chapter	13.	Waak Good	120
Chapter	14.	The Nanny's Irie	138
Chapter	15.	The Society of Jamaican Nanny Boys	148
Chapter	16.	The Aftermath	160
Chapter	17.	One Blood	176
Chapter	18.	Redemption Psalm	187
Acknowledgements			193

1. As It Was in the Beginning

When I reflect on Dezna's power over the twelve years she raised me, seared into my mind is this singular image: a vermilion cotton jersey, rumpled on the floor, with "Foxy's" scribbled across the front in white Lucida calligraphy. All that time with her in Princeton, New Jersey, and my mind veers magnetically towards that night.

The evening in question, Thursday, September 26, 1991 – when I'm a few weeks into kindergarten – begins with the calmness of Indian summer in the Garden State. Newly extinguished citronella candles smoke in wisps on the patio, and glass-of-lemonade light floods the backyard in a way that seems to ensure peace far past dusk.

At the kitchen table, I hold my finished "homework link", a math problem on a half sheet of loose-leaf. I have circled the answer on the scrap in pencil.

"Let's see, Maas Ross," Dezna says, placing a Pyrex dish on a trivet and moving away from the stove where she is preparing dinner – scalloping potatoes into a colander.

ANOTHER MOTHER

"Maas," that old Jamaican word of respect – the one whose significance I don't quite get, the one she applies facetiously to a *pickney* when it's reserved for the aged and wise.

Dezna tucks her seashell-pink house dress under the backs of her knees as she sits at the table with me to check over my work. She has thin lips she knits together in an expectant fashion, and her nerdy glasses rest on her bridgeless nose, which descends to a bulbous tip.

She squints her almond-shaped eyes and confirms my steps are correct, that the final answer is right. Then she sings, as always, a little ditty:

> *Good, better, best*
> *Never let it rest*
> *'Til your good becomes your better*
> *And your better becomes your best...*

... That's right, Ras-mon.

There is formulaic order to this exercise, snatched out of my household's natural state: chaos.

Just then, the back door slams as my father returns from his hardware store and enters the mud room at five o'clock on the dot. He lumbers into the kitchen, his broad shoulders giving way to a limber physique. A former fat kid and high school football kicker who churned the flub into lean muscle through a running habit, he appears as a marathon-ready Larry David in a plaid button-down and Dockers.

"Irv," my mother says, bounding into the kitchen from the den and looking at her Movado watch. "Why are you *testing* me?" She's five-five and lissom, her hair an auburn achieved through frequent salon visits. Her face and shoulders are tanned and freckly from a childhood spent at the Jersey Shore. She stands bevelled, her right foot forward with the heel raised – equally ready to pounce or receive a passed canapé. I watch this interplay with a strained brow, as my curly-haired older sister, Nicole, a Fraggle-ish Shirley Temple who is seven, sock-slides into the kitchen.

"I had to take care of some things at the store, Cindy," he improvises, slipping on careless, slurred s's as he places a brown paper bag atop the counter – the bottle inside ringing in a dull echo against the Formica.

"O.K., tell Dr Galietta that when we're late."

My father hits the counter with his fist, and my mother gets up in his face.

"*Cho!*" Dezna says, a patois exclamation of disgust. My parents freeze, and Dezna scrunches up her nose, raising her lips to her nostrils as if smelling something old in the fridge. "Not before the children," she says.

I move from the kitchen to the downstairs half-bath and begin a familiar routine amid this discord. I go to the Delta sink and turn on the right handle for cold water. I pass my left hand under the tap so that the stream touches my palm first and then guide my hand to allow the water to trace the length of my middle finger for a symmetrical path. I mirror the gesture with my right hand. Then I tap the sink handle with my right middle finger, skim the right side of my nose with that same finger, touch my right hip, hit the top of my right foot, press the pudgy tip of my middle finger into the floor, and then begin the washing sequence again. I complete this process a total of four times before twisting the sink handle shut and exiting the bathroom on my right foot. My knuckles bloody if I so much as clench my fist.

"Nicole, Ross – we'll be back soon," my mother yells from the back hall as I exit the bathroom. "Do what Dezna tells you to. She's in charge."

"Love-a you," I call out.

"Love-a you," Nicole says.

"Ras-mon, Nicole, come sit yuh dung – lez *nyam* our deener," Dezna sings. "Unu don't want to be late for our shows."

Dezna nourishes us with red snapper, cheesy potatoes, and ginger beer. The meal she has prepared, as always, lacks pork or shellfish. Our Jewish household essentially kept kosher throughout the '90s, because Dezna's Seventh-day Adventist sumptuary laws mirrored Jewish restrictions. The mere mention of shrimp would cause Dezna to scrunch up her nose.

The rest of the night will unfold, we think, in a typical manner: we'll watch our seven o'clock *Jeopardy!* and 7:30 *Wheel of Fortune* before getting ready for bed come eight o'clock. Because of my paranoia about robbers and bandits, dybbuks and duppies, I'll go to sleep in the extra twin bed in Nicole's room, with its pink colour scheme that turns Creamsicle when Dezna dims the lights.

After dinner, my sister perches on the den's Persian rug and immerses herself in a new game she calls "Nicole Solitaire", one that involves scattering a deck of cards according to inscrutable rules. Dezna and I watch, look at each other, observe some more as Nicole – donning her customary shoulder-padded blazer, a staple of hers throughout elementary school – curiously orders her world.

"You wouldn't understand," Nicole says when I ask how the game works. I am only five and a quarter, after all.

But this flippancy is confusing, because this is my sister, whose birthday cards always include cheery acrostics: ROSS – RAD, OUTSTANDING, SMART, SPORTY. This is my sister, the positive child, who thinks death doesn't belong in music; when Don McLean's "American Pie" comes on the radio, she alters the lyrics to sing, *"This'll be the day that I live. This'll be the day that I live."* And yet, no answers.

Soon enough, Nicole and I invade Dezna's quarters – the room redolent of the castor oil she uses on her Marcelled hair. Amid the modest surroundings – coral-pink carpeting, a twin bed, an old JVC TV, a rummage-sale wardrobe, a sliding-door closet, a sewing table – a whole universe exists. I am wearing a red T-Shirt from Foxy's, a bar on Jost Van Dyke Island in the Caribbean, where my grandfather would sail. The soft, cotton-poly blend souvenir is so long I can wear it alone over tighty-whities as a nightshirt.

"This. Is. *Jeopardy!*" says Johnny Gilbert, the show's famed announcer – a statement that could also characterise my home environment. I pull the red Foxy's shirt over my knees as I sit on the floor and hug my legs. The sky through the windows is the blue of Boardwalk and Park Place.

ANOTHER MOTHER

Though our little trinity in front of Alex Trebek's game operates with tranquillity, my parents' typical tension stands in stark contrast – a tenor foretold in their very first meeting.

∗∗∗

It is the fall of 1981, and Sheryl, a mutual friend of my parents' living in Princeton, has brought my mother, then thirty, to Witherspoon Street downtown to meet my father. My mother, who has an '80s feminist predilection for wearing YSL pantsuits, also has an awkwardness that, despite her put-togetherness, prompts her to begin all encounters with a too-earnest "Hiya!" She doesn't expect much during her first visit to the hardware store, and as she spies my father through the vitrine, she notes his handsome profile is gaunt and beschnozzed like that of a deposed count. When, after a moment's pause, she enters the shop – a shabby establishment with screws loose in bins – she has an immediate distaste for the curly-haired man behind the counter chewing Juicy Fruit gum and shooting one-liners to customers: jokes about golf, heaven, erections.

"What is this, some kind of haberdashery?" she says, taking her customary ALL-CAPS approach to communication. My father believes he has zero chance.

"So, you're *Ir*vin *U*rken?" she says, emphasising the awkward alliteration of his name. My mother holds in her smirk until it bursts into a mini giggle.

My father's jokes occupy a particular space in the comedic genre that relies on wit so intentionally bad you can't but sigh – groaners about boners, mostly. He could have been something in the Borscht Belt. This tendency extends from a place of social insecurity, to run interference on real conversation. He'd attribute this to the fact that his father died of a heart attack on Halloween night when he was ten years old; his mother, Eunice, shut off all the lights in their brick house on Nassau Street across from the synagogue to ward off trick-or-treaters. They sat there in the living room with his father's dead body in silence, a quiet that would characterise the rest of his home life. The yearning for an audience inspired this performative tendency that doubled as emotional distancing. There's no need to confront reality – in a marriage, say – if the formulaic quip is just a sentence away. All this is perhaps inevitable for a man whose last name rhymes with "merkin."

With a blizzard set to blanket this hallowed Jersey community and people rushing to buy snow shovels at Urken's, he might offer, in reference to his future wife, "Princeton isn't the only thing getting eight to ten inches tonight." *Rimshot!*

Throughout her twenties, my mother insists she will marry a nice Jewish doctor or lawyer: someone upstanding in society, a mensch. Certainly not a manila folder-complexioned Cyrano who sells sprocket wrenches. After all, my mother is from Neptune – Neptune, New Jersey – toward the wuddery parts of the state where her father started a tomato business from dust – stood at his Englishtown flea market food cart on fall days and desiccated Julys so he could buy property, then a packinghouse, then a life, and then a Cadillac. He became a tomato magnate and named the tomato company Cindy Brand Tomatoes after my mother. Bruce Springsteen was a year ahead of her at Freehold

ANOTHER MOTHER

High and called her Cindy Tomato. My grandfather moved his family to a modest manse and bought acres of tomato land in Sarasota, Florida – fields of promise. My mother, then, was something of an heirloom heiress.

Somehow, my father's spirit won over her prim hauteur, but it was my mother's parents – while living, and later through a bequest – who allowed her to embrace a chichi lifestyle. In the summer of 1988 as her family of four demanded more space, they bought her the large house on Hale Drive in Princeton, a place run rampant with Bermuda shorts, Top-Siders, liberal ideals, and critter ties among the nattering nabobs of Nassau. The children there participated in equestrian show-jumping and interpretive archery, and among adults, Lilly Pulitzer outfits were as common as Pulitzer Prizes. Not everyone could handle the pervasive preppiness, of course; some suffered what my father called Lacoste intolerance. But in a non-showy way, the Chevy SUV parents in town drove during my childhood neatly branded the entire lifestyle: Suburban. My grandparents provided my mother with the means for fancy Caribbean vacations to the Ritz-Carlton at Rose Hall in Montego Bay or spa days at Elizabeth Arden in New York City. It was the money that would allow for her children's elite private school and Ivy League educations, along with a live-in Jamaican nanny. My father's hardware store didn't generate the cash to afford these upper middle-class appurtenances – it couldn't even pay the mortgage – and my mother inherently resented the arrangement. She memorised the corporate titles of other Princeton men – "Global Head of Sales," she'd recite – and kept tabs on where other families vacationed and who got such and such a bonus. My mother stewed and found release in binge trips to T.J. Maxx and Marshalls, followed by jugular-flared yelling.

All happy families are alike. But then you have the Urkens. My mother's complaints became a policy of Absolutism – that is, driving my father to Absolut vodka. Sometimes it was the fifth of Appleton rum Dezna brought him when returning from Jamaica.

***

I've pulled the Foxy's shirt over my knees in a way that makes it look like I have huge breasts if I lean back and stretch the fabric. The back edge of the shirt is secured under my batty, all the more so as I'm sitting on my hands.

Jeopardy! is in full swing, and Dezna excels at the "Word Origins" category.

"From the Old French for 'crib,' it's a representation of a nativity scene," says Trebek.

"What is 'crèche'?" Dezna says nonchalantly. One hundred dollars.

"From Old English for 'One that breaks faith,' it's a male witch," says Trebek.

"What is 'warlock'?" Dezna says. Two hundred dollars.

"This term for a little angel often depicted as a rosy-cheeked child comes from Hebrew," Trebek says.

I look over at Dezna, expectantly. I gaze up at her face, at her cheekbones the perfect roundness of Dome Poppers –

those rubber half-spheres that launch from a table top – her nose scroonched up, and those heavy-lidded abacus-bead eyes, ancient and ever calculating.

"What is 'cherub'?" Three hundred dollars.

Nicole, Dezna, and I slap five. We're pumped. My ears are overflowing with the intoxicating rhythm of Dezna's language. Any tension fades into oblivion. This evening is about solving problems with correct answers. This evening is about victory. It's us against the world.

Next up is America's game, *Wheel of Fortune*. Though the previous half hour hinged on trivia and intelligence, this game relies less on one's abilities, more on luck. Kismet can alter your station in an instant. Where you end up has less to do with your hard work and more with the hand you are dealt at the wheel. Chance is in charge.

There is half an hour to get through before bedtime. The evening is strung together so seamlessly. And Vanna White is in a stunning sequined dress.

"Ya, mon – Vanna *rayal* – like a queen," Dezna says.

The vowels are for sale on TV, but in our Jamaican-tinged bavardage, they are shortened, flattened, deepened. The three of us shout, "C'mon, big money!" Dezna solves the puzzles, and Nicole and I lavish in our collective victory, some two or three spins before the contestants on the tube.

Dezna is keeping everything in order – this woman who appeared during a blizzard on our porch that one February day in 1988 when I was eighteen months. Smartly bemillinered, she carried a carpetbag and seemed to have blown in from the East Wind. She may not have been the person my mother anticipated when her friend's au pair recommended a nanny – one my mother hoped would also be European – but my mother was desperate after a previous nanny let our basement flood while on a personal phone call.

"So…remind me where you're from again, Haiti?" my mother said that day, perhaps at least hopeful for her children's French-language immersion.

"Jamaica."

"Oh, *Jamaica*, O.K. – and you left to come to this?" my mother said, indicating the snow drifts in the backyard. "I've been to Jamaica, and if you put me on a plane there today, I might never come back."

***

Every Thursday, Nicole and I stay with Dezna while our parents have "date night" to address their issues. Evenings with Dezna. I interpret this as time for levelling off, smoothing over, *evening*.

My parents' screaming matches are inevitable, as most marital relationships turn martial when couples team up professionally. At the hardware store during business hours, my mother offers her two cents on the design side of the shop with window treatment and wall paper sales on a part-time basis. Arguments escalate during recessions, and the grade of retail sales can predict my family's collective sanity. As part of my parents' underlying rift, the hardware shop falls victim to the encroaching big-box stores in the '90s. My father sneers and alters the spelling of his powerful chain-corporation competition: Home Despot. He has the keys to the whole world, or at least the metal Baldwin blanks for our whole town. At his key-cutting machine, he shapes jagged teeth as gold filings pile up as shiny dust on the counter. The irony that this store, where other families shop for supplies to support their homes, cannot sustain our own household is not lost on us. My paternal grandfather, a Latvian transplant to Princeton, had started the business as a glass shop – perhaps a more earnest expression of retail's fragility. And as with retail, marriage.

My mercurial mother and my father, skilled in the dark arts of passive-aggressiveness, lack the ability to resolve their disputes. I spend many rheumy evenings shouting from my bedroom, "Stop yelling!" I retreat often into the bathroom to wash my hands.

In the upstairs of the hardware store, there is a cot my father uses on nights my parents' fights fly off the rails. He spends a lot of time on that bed. Sometimes we drive up there to fetch him and find him lying on the ground by the register.

As if subject to tectonic tension, my parents' relationship is prone to give way eventually. But Dezna counterpushes, attenuates their antagonism. The fights tend to break out come evening, so my anxiety level shifts according to the position of the sun. During the worst of moments, Dezna wades into the trenches to defuse the argument before the destruction intensifies. *Cho.* This consistent feat stands among the acts that ultimately canonise Dezna's sainthood in our household. She plays referee to these well-intentioned but unstable people a decade younger and gets in between them when their anger entangles them physically in shoves and swipes. "Count to ten," she says "*Shhh.*"

Similar to the devil sticks I played with that were in vogue at the time, our house followed the metronomic tick-tock of balance with Dezna around. But in her absence, one hiccup during a vulnerable move could drop the baton of stability to the floor.

One Saturday evening, I am watching the Stanley Cup finals in which the Avalanche would eventually sweep the Florida Panthers. My fingertips are coated in Cheetos dust, and I let forth a Barq's root beer burp. It is the weekend, and with Nicole out at a sleepover and Dezna back in West Orange (her Seventh-day Adventist Sabbath, like the Jewish one, is on Saturday), I am left alone with my parents.

As usual, their skirmish intensifies, and amid the body checks on-screen, I hear the slam of my father's fist on the ground of the playroom – a bash of frustration, as if hitting the steering wheel with the heel of his palm after missing an exit. My mother's arguing technique centres on whingeing and wearing my father down so he'll admit he did something wrong, usually an incident more than a decade ago. In this case, his misdeed is taking out a loan from his mother to buy the hardware store instead of letting my mother's father buy it for him outright.

"It was an idiotic and selfish decision to go ahead and buy the store yourself," she says. "Now, what am I saying?"

ANOTHER MOTHER

"You're saying you think I made a stupid decision to buy the store alone," my dad says, lying slumped on the floor with his head resting against the cold door leading to the garage.

"And what did I say ten years ago?" my mother says. "I said, 'Irv, pursue me. Pursue me.'"

"You know what, Cindy?" my dad says. "You're right." That's his go-to tactic – telling my mother her points are valid in a voice that nonetheless conveys his actual disagreement. That riles my mother up all the more.

"Oh, I'm right?" she says. "I'm *right?*"

Their therapy and self-help books don't seem to guide them towards a compatible cruising altitude. Without Dezna around to intervene, their fight soon intensifies. My father makes for the back door to take a drive to the store, and my mother gets in front of him. He brushes past her, leading with his shoulder, and slams the back door, at which point I run from the den through the kitchen to the back hall, where I see my mother sitting with a bloody nose (a single raspberry syrup drop has fallen to the floor) and my father looking through the back-door window, illuminated by the porchlight, his face alabaster.

He didn't mean for that to happen, tried to get out of the situation. He's outside and opens the door halfway. He sees my mother crying through the pane.

"Are you O.K.?" I say. "Do you need to go to the hospital?"

"I'm fine," my mother says through tears.

"Come in here – she's bleeding."

My father sulks back in, sucking quick breaths. He tries to help my mother up, but she shoos him off.

I hear the squeak of the liquor cabinet in the living room, then his trudge upstairs to sleep in Nicole's room for the night. My mother collects herself and, dismissing conversation, kisses me on the forehead and holds me in a hug. I feel one of her single warm tears on my cheek. She ascends the stairs to her room, a hallway from my father.

***

"I'll give the wheel a final spin and ask you to give me a letter," Pat Sajak says. "If it's in the puzzle, you have three seconds to solve it. Vowels are worth nothing. Consonants are worth...."

That means the day is about to end. Dezna will make us "brush and flush" and "go yuh bed."

But I don't want it to end. Fuelled by an extra burst of energy here with bedtime fast approaching, I am hopping around. I am jumping like crazy.

"*Rudie, rudie, rudie come from jail...*," Dezna sings, another typical strategy from her to warn I am testing her. "You're acting like a leggo beas'."

She turns around, her back now to me: "Laad, give mi strenkt."

I keep jumping there in my Foxy's T-shirt, pilly with the white Lucida calligraphy silk screening paint cracked from the heat of the dryer. I climb on Dezna's bed and begin jumping some more. She turns to face me.

"What-a joke to you is death to me," Dezna warns, with that catch in her voice.

But my excitement is unhinged. I am bouncing around the mattress.

ANOTHER MOTHER

Suddenly, I launch myself from the bed, and Nicole, fearing that I'm about to land off balance, intercepts me. She is trying to catch me around the waist and place me down gently, but instead, to Dezna's horror across the room, she grabs too low on my hamstrings and sends the top half of my body flying backward toward the ground. The coral-pink carpet draws closer as gravity deals with my body. I bear the brunt of the impact with my right wrist, which twists on the fall.

Dezna sees me plummet from across the room, hears the snap, and jolts over to inspect the damage – gently embracing me and elevating my arm, running her hand soothingly through my hair. I am yelping in intermittent high-pitched squeals.

"Hushhh – hushhh, Ras-mon," Dezna says.

She goes through a checklist of her medical questions, investigating my range of motion and pain tolerance.

"It's just a fracture," Dezna says, with her thumb and middle finger circled around my wrist.

"Ross, forgive?" Nicole says as I cry. "Forgive?"

"Come-yuh, Ras-mon," Dezna says.

Dezna wants extra guidance, so she starts to ferry me across the street to the house of Dr Garland, a cardiologist whose family appropriately keeps a Christmas wreath up year-round. She knows our neighbours from the bus stop, where she stands in contrast to the other adults (the kids on the bus ask me: "Who is that lady waving to you?"). The cul-de-sac neighbourhood, called Heatherstone, and our street in particular, Hale Drive, named for the patriot Nathan Hale, are an elaborate rendering of homogeneity beyond the oyster-shell driveways. There is an array of Princeton professors, men who commute to finance jobs in New York, doctors, and other white-collar professionals. Most of the mothers are of the stay-at-home variety but otherwise preoccupied with committees, community- or charity-oriented. Though there is some ethnic diversity, a few Chinese families and one of Pakistani origins, Dezna is the only black person in the development.

We amble through the dewy grass, italicised in the wind – past the floodlights, the pointy yuccas, the tussocks, the Japanese maple, and the weeping cherry, as Nicole waits by our open front door, an illuminated yellow rectangle that the black of night surrounds.

At the house of Dr Garland, I hold my arm out for him as the blue light of the TV squiggles through the hallway. He suggests I wait until the morning to get an X-ray and treatment from an orthopaedist.

Upon arriving back at our house across the lawn, Dezna sets up a makeshift mini-clinic in my bedroom. I have thrown off my T-shirt and sit Silly-Puttied on my knock-off Eames chair bought at Sam's Club, amid my football wallpaper and a framed Leroy Neiman Roger Staubach lithograph. She dives into her sewing kits, snatching out choice fabrics to fashion a sling, and binds muslin with taffeta before affixing a velveteen cushion to my elbow. Trained as a nurse and a seamstress, she excels at remedying this mishap. She sets an ice pack on my wrist and holds it firm, muttering some healing incantation. I do not ask much but take comfort in knowing she can make the pain go away. I don't mind being shushed or there-there'd.

ANOTHER MOTHER

Dezna calls for a warm washcloth from Nicole, like a TV doctor for a scalpel. She places it on my forehead and fetches a leather dopp kit with various vials and calabash containers filled with oils, balms, and unguents. Dabbing a dollop of aloe vera which she calls sinkle bible on a cotton swab, she applies the goo to my wrist.

Dezna is similarly skilled with splinters. She handles scraped knees with aplomb, specialises in boo-boos. As I calm down, she brushes my bangs back from my forehead and serves me cerasee, a bitter tea panacea.

She swaddles me as she tucks me in and sings:

> Red and yellow, black and white,
> Jesus loves the Israelite
> Jesus loves the little children of the world.

The next day will solve everything, Dezna assures me: "Erryting will be fine *inna di morrows.*"

She starts to sing another ditty:

> Carry mi ackee go a Linstead Market
> Not a quattie wut sell
> Carry mi ackee go a Linstead Market
> Not a quattie wut sell

The dimmed lights wince overhead. My Foxy's T-shirt is still rumpled in the corner. Dezna picks it up as she sings and, with superhuman swiftness, folds it into a creaseless square.

2. Of Melodies Pure and True

One morning a little more than a month before she moves to New Jersey, a woman leans on the banister of her cedar veranda and peers out at the breadfruit trees – trying to find peace. This is the home that, until the day before, the forty-six-year-old shared with her husband of twenty-one years here in Pisgah, deep in the heart of Jamaica's St Elizabeth parish.

She runs her pointer finger along her tear ducts expecting moisture but realises they've gone dry. Her eyes are a warm nougat, and she places her Coke-bottle glasses back on over her almost bridgeless nose. She refastens a copper butterfly brooch on the pink linen dress she sewed herself. This woman, Dezna Sanderson, Miss Dezna if you care to be proper, takes a sip of her bush tea and sighs in consonance with the petchary's song. It's July 1987 – one of the hottest months the island has seen in a decade – and she sits down, long-necked, stately on a cedar throne like an abbess. You might not know it to look at her, but she's in mourning – jutting her impudent chin and taking in her new reality.

ANOTHER MOTHER

Yesterday, Dezna's husband, George Sanderson, after two decades of tending his fields, had keeled over while bumping papayas down from the trees with a twelve-ounce Ting bottle rigged to a broom shaft. Known as Bready, a portly, five-three Smee of a man, he suffered a massive coronary, and Dezna went looking for him when he didn't come in for a lunch of steamed red snapper.

"George?" she called, throwing her dishrag next to the sink. "Georg, come yuh...."

She sauntered through the nearest pineapple grove, past discarded sardine tins, to find Bready taking a nap, surely, among the fallen palm fronds. His face was lodged in the reddish, bauxite-rich silt of the farmland.

"Georgie!"

It was moments later when she yelled for help from her kids – the youngest two of eight still at home, her daughters Carla and Fabi, twelve and eleven – that she came to a realisation: she couldn't stay here any longer. In a tumultuous life, she knew well enough that such tragedies were unpredictable. "Trouble nuh set like rain," she said to her girls. She'd have to change course.

Dezna's relationship with George had begun with such promise when they met in Mahogany Hill on April 26, 1966, the same day Ethiopian Emperor Haile Selassie visited Kingston before a crowd of a hundred thousand Rastas. Just twenty-five years old and already the mother of three sons, Dezna had moved from Montego Bay back to St Elizabeth with her parents and soon thereafter began to work as a clinician for the

Jamaican Ministry of Health. Every day, she walked the steep path to work from Mahogany Hill to Ginger Hill – expansive pineapple groves as far as the eye could see and bougainvillea and frangipani patched throughout the shrubbery. Here at the edge of Cockpit Country, the land was lush and reliable. The thrum of optimism emanated from Jamaica, newly independent from British rule. Miss Dezna – shod in a pair of moccasins and outfitted in one of the polka dot dresses she'd designed – would sashay her way into villages to make house calls, nurse the elderly, and counsel young men and women on the importance of condoms. All the while, she'd hear the admiration of the planters and the miners – her dress cinched tight to accentuate her hips.

"Hafftanoon, Miss Dezna," they'd call.

"Good heevlin, Miss Dezna," they'd say, and whistle.

Miss Dezna bounded up the hills and, with her medicine bag in hand and a spring in her defined calves, emitted a shy laugh. She strode across the ridges, eczamaed red with the bauxite debris. She felt purposeful, and in her veins pumped a belief that just maybe it would be possible to build a beautiful life here.

One day when making a house call to a squat bachelor thirteen years her senior – a *fawma*, specialising in pineapples – she provided him with some tablets to lower his blood pressure. "O.K., Mistah Sanderson," she said, giving his knee two staccato taps before her customary goodbye: "Likkle more…blessings…"

He smelled like musk and had a trim, grizzled beard, she noticed. It was stuffy in his dwelling – too hot, she mentioned.

ANOTHER MOTHER

"Otta outside...," he said.

She patted his thigh one more time. In the heat of the moment, though, and against her nursely intentions, his heart beat faster, and there in his little hut, they exchanged a slow kiss.

"Wa'ppun?" she said, startled by what just occurred.

She paused, then removed her Coke-bottle glasses and leaned in to embrace him.

No, no, she thought. Not this again. She wasn't ready for it. Not after what she'd been through.

The father of her first child woke up one morning eight years earlier and told her he'd booked passage on a ship to England; he left that afternoon as tears streamed down her eighteen-year-old face. *Nuh leave me*, she said. *Please, nuh leave me.* And just last year marked the end of her relationship with the father of her second and third sons; the squabbling drove her to abandon her tidy life in Montego Bay and head back to country. And yet, here was this pot-bellied charmer.

"You think you came here by accident?" he said.

She twisted her mouth to one side in protest and beamed at him – slightly impressed by his arrogance.

George and Dezna married that year and had Maxine, the first of their five children together, in 1967. They moved *dung di rohd* to nearby Pisgah in 1969, with Dezna's three sons in tow. George wanted to focus on his pineapples here where the groves dominated the landscape and clumps of houses, some little more than lean-tos, stood on the hillside.

The Taíno, the indigenous tribe of the Caribbean, originally brought pineapples to Jamaica from South America, and to provide for his family, George would grow the different varietals – Cowboy, Ripley, Sugar Loaf. Pineapples represented abundance and hospitality, and they even emblazoned the Red Cross on the Jamaican Coat of Arms. This life, if not one of plenty, brought enough joy – with Dezna often tending to a big pudding pan of Jamaican black cake on the wood fireplace or making gizzada, a coconut pastry also known as a pinch-me-round, while the children played cricket in the road or dandy shandy by the sweetgum tree. There were nights of ska and dub parties – the Sandersons had the best radio in the village. No trouble, Dezna thought, couldn't be danced away. She closed her eyes when she swayed, nuzzling into George, sturdy as a banyan tree.

On that knotty cedar veranda, Dezna, her daughters would later note, sits staring wide-eyed into the vegetation, the paunched hills rising in the distance. She imagines an uncertain future with her past dramatically toppled. Dezna realises the tragic path here resulted from the gradual erosion of her life's righteous shores. First, there wasn't much to fuss over, just years of hunger. A little more than a decade after its 1962 independence from the British, Jamaica had to borrow immensely from the International Monetary Fund, which tightened its belt on the economy. The disappointments did not dissipate the populace's long-clung-to optimism, and their upbeat attitude seemed to manifest in the name of one of the capital city's famous thoroughfares: Old Hope Road. The farther you were from Kingston, of course, the less you had.

ANOTHER MOTHER

As she sips her steaming cup of bush tea, Dezna thinks back to the ultimate irony: in a nation rich with sugarcane, the Sandersons in remote Pisgah couldn't even get sugar in their household for tea and had to ration maple syrup to drizzle into mugs. The resources in the country were choked, and power outages became the norm. But they still had a modest pineapple business and some papayas.

That is, until the CIA's infiltration of Jamaica in the 1970s put an end to that steadiness in Dezna's family. Left-wing Prime Minister Michael Manley of the People's National Party (PNP) grew close to Fidel Castro, and paranoia mounted that the island would go red. The Sandersons went about their routines – the kids at school, Dezna at house calls, Bready in the fields – but the US government wanted to prevent Jamaica from becoming another banana republic. So it launched a covert military operation in 1976 that enveloped the island, subtly at first like the sennit fringe of coral reef that surrounds Jamaica. The CIA's Jamaica station chief Norman Descoteaux tightened his influence on the island and ran a destabilisation programme with the ultimate goal of installing Edward Seaga of the Jamaica Labour Party (JLP) as prime minister. Operation Condor was in full flight throughout Latin America, and tiny Jamaica got wrapped up in the mix.

Time is tropical – that is, unpredictable.

And the elongated calm of uneventful years can vanish in an instant. The once-even tempo grew frenetic for the Sandersons, and it became hard to find the right beat amid discord. The political chaos increased and washed away their halcyon days.

Just as he had discredited Salvador Allende in Chile, President Richard Nixon wanted to subvert the Manley government. The best way to do that? "Make the economy scream," said Tricky Dick as Jamaicans maligned the island's "politricks". A hairline fissure appeared on Dezna's brow, a vertical strain from the tension her nation gathered and redistributed to her family and others – in the form of less opportunity and more violence. Poor Georgie, trying to provide, suffered the consequences too, and as the national mayhem lapped away at this Land of Wood and Water, the plaque buildup in his arteries grew. Fortunes too quickly curdled into misfortunes.

The CIA's plan involved a complicated and stealthy operation: assassinations, the funnelling of money to the JLP, and arms distribution to PNP enemies like the notorious Lester "Jim Brown" Coke and his Shower Posse. Dezna's Jamaica was under siege, pumped with heroin, cocaine, cheap arms, death squads, gang violence. *Come to Jamaica and feel all right.* Bullet holes dimpled walls. The CIA had to wreck the economy from the inside out as Communist fear remained pervasive. The whole scheme hit agricultural exports hard, particularly pineapples, dealing Dezna's family a blow. And even Bob Marley's 1978 One Love Peace Concert at the National Stadium, in which the icon held hands with political rivals Seaga and Manley, brought only short-lived order. The country became politically volatile, and the campaign leading up to the 1980 election between Seaga and Manley scattered some eight hundred murders across the island, with the CIA arming ghettos and encouraging makeshift militias to wield influence over the democratic process. Automatic rifles, silencers, and ammunition poured into Jamaica. Pineapples meant less than grenades.

While the kids went to school, Dezna pushed on through and joined a team of sister nurses travelling through the hills to promote Western medicine at a time when ganja was exploding and people still widely practised obeah and myal, African-Caribbean forms of magic and syncretic belief systems. She had a vegetable scale for weighing babies on which she assessed each *pickney* of the hills. Every other Friday, pristinely clothed in polka dot dresses or black pencil skirts with ruffled white blouses, Dezna went to Black River for a Ministry of Health conference. Her house became a makeshift hospital by day and a dance hall by night. She ventured into the villages to treat the ill, and when the patients couldn't pay her cash, she came back home with her pockets stuffed full of yam and parsnips. She had to feed her eight children and couldn't refuse.

Her kids collected bottles for recycling – "picking," they called it – to help the family make ends meet. But the country at large suffered, with declining agricultural exports and nearly half the population unemployed. George continued to harvest the pineapples and load them onto trucks from companies like GraceKennedy to be brought to Kingston and sold or shipped internationally. But fewer trucks came, and they paid less and less.

The vertical fissure on Dezna's brow deepened. The sediment in George's arteries accumulated. Jamaica's unrest rose to a fever pitch.

And then George collapsed onto that soil he so long used to build up a life.

The ebony tree in the yard had just flowered, and per Jamaican legend, would soon bring on downpours.

Sitting like a queen in the morning breeze on the knotty cedar veranda – the one known to prick children with grey-green fingertip splinters – Dezna is at a loss, having stitched a life that feels fully unravelled. She is now a widow. She knows she can't farm pineapples all by herself and provide for her family, and here waiting to prepare for her husband's nine-night mourning feast, she confirms what she must do.

With her sister Rohena already in New York, she decides she'll try to make a life for herself in the United States where nurses can earn plenty more than at home. Selling trinkets at the higgler cart, going into MoBay to hawk "Ya mon" tchotchkes won't put adequate food on the table. Miss Dezna must *go farrin'*.

America will be her future. The United States of America will welcome the tired, the poor lady. Of course, she doesn't know exactly what she'll do, but she's always found a way to make it work. She can let her oldest children watch over her pre-teen daughters while she sends home remittances. It's not ideal to abandon those girls at this age, but considerations of right and wrong are irrelevant; this is about survival. A little more than twenty years from now, though she of course doesn't know it, she will return here for good.

Dezna reflects back on her days with Bready – so deceivingly innocent – now nothing more than sweet memories. Come

ANOTHER MOTHER

September, she'll take her first-ever flight from Jamaica to JFK in Jamaica, Queens, to stay with her sister and brother-in-law. Some months later she'll end up in a university town she'd never heard of, watching two children who would become like her own.

Just now Carla and Fabi, their hair in cornrows, run out to Dezna's cedar throne – wailing over their father. Who's going to keep them in line during their whispered *laba laba* at the Seventh-day Adventist church? Or walk with them for a cold Ting, that fizzy grapefruit elixir, and an *arinj* at the drink shack? And if their mother leaves, who will go to wash with them up by YS Falls in the frigid stream? Who will sing "Hill an' Gully Rider" or pull their hair tight to fasten their braids with bubble clips that are like mini nunchucks? Who will cut up a ripe jackfruit?

The girls hug their mother, dotting her dress with their warm tears, and she pulls them in closer – one enveloped in each arm. She gets up and guides them back into the house.

"Mummy always here fi you," Dezna says. "Mummy nuh leave you."

3. Miss Dezna

*I*t was a supreme role reversal as I sat next to Dezna's bed in Newark's Beth Israel Hospital, feeding her Kozy-Shack rice pudding and wiping the residue from her lips. Tucked in her sheets, she looked dignified as ever. But her skin had lost its glow, her cheekbones jutted, and her eyes mustered merely a glassy squint.

No longer a *pickney* with an auburn bowl cut and a neon green cast on my fractured right wrist, I was instead an unruly-haired twenty-something – my beard a rabbinical Brillo. Nicole and I stood in seeming contrast to the others in Dezna's hospital room – the Caribbean churchwomen from her Seventh-day Adventist congregation who sang hymns, held my hands, and told me of Jesus. Although I appeared a distinct outsider, I knew I could reveal our surprising shared identity simply by opening my mouth. Because unlike most Jewish boys from New Jersey, I have a Jamaican accent.

Throughout my life, I have faced guffaws of incredulity and pshaws of dismissal when I explain my unusual inflection doesn't reflect the influence of my native Princeton or the musicality of Torah tropes, but rather the singsong lilt of the West Indies, the hum-drum of Jamaican hillside chatter, the modulated thump of reggae. But that's the honest-to-goodness truth, and it all started with Dezna.

Though most kids of my generation in Jersey first experienced the Jamaican accent solely through Sebastian, the bombastic crab from *The Little Mermaid*, I did not confine my own exposure to "unda da sea." Dezna's island influence permeated my upbringing, from her patois expressions that rattled my eardrums to her ackee and salt fish breakfasts.

But beyond cultural osmosis, Dezna played a much larger role: she maintained order in our household, one plagued by addiction and mental illness. Smashed glasses, slammed doors served as the cacophonous codas to my parents' arguments. My father's mom-and-pop hardware store, where Einstein once had a charge account, had fallen from grace as business slowed in the '90s. My mother expressed her disappointment in bipolar rage episodes, which certainly did not lessen my father's desire to seek therapeutic comfort in drink.

Depakote, Lithium, Klonopin – my mother took those pills to keep her chemical imbalance in check. Absolut, Beefeater, Stolichnaya – those became my father's self-prescribed medications.

And still: the chasing around the kitchen table, my mother's habit of dumping my father's clothes at the end of the driveway, my father's own retaliatory gesture of packing his belongings in a trunk and dragging it down the stairs (scraping the wood on the landing). Dezna's role hinged on preserving calm for Nicole and me in a household always on the verge of combustion. She kept everything *irie*, a term I wouldn't understand until years later.

Dezna, when returning from a weekend away, would smooth over the cracks – her strength employed as emotional spackle within the Urken house. It was indeed the tension between my mother and father that drove me to appreciate the stability she provided, the necessary third leg of our family's parental tripod. In the equation of my homelife, Dezna was a constant, my parents variables. And so I sought placidity in Dezna's warmth, her honeyed tympanic voice, wholesome food, and healing abilities. Her evenness largely enabled my own, against all odds – this second mother eating sardines and reading the Bible at seven in the morning, yelling at the TV come evening with her "dohn go in deer, gyal" admonishments, calling me something closer to "Ras" than "Ross".

Throughout my childhood, though, I still sought to make order out of entropy by myself, and handwashing became my go-to refuge. I could stand at the bathroom sink for half an hour straight to perform OCD rituals that stressed symmetry and repetition; the world around me might have been in chaos, but I felt purified, my knuckles bloodied and all. That behaviour intensified only after Dezna moved out following my bar mitzvah when my parents determined I no longer needed a nanny. (My father dubbed this "the end of the age of ironing.") Without Dezna to keep my parents in order and my anxiety at bay, my mind and body conspired against me with panic attacks. In a frantic search for resolution, my mother sent me to no fewer than half a dozen therapists in the surrounding towns and states to find it. There was Dr Schnapps, an Israeli doctor who assured me Prozac would reduce my compulsions; Dr Sharlin, out in Pennsylvania, who had me try to stand in front of my bathroom sink for an hour at a time without washing my hands ("Confront the faucet..."); and Dr Gursky, who prescribed Trileptal, Lexapro, and Xanax when I started having fits of hyperventilation so severe I had to blow into brown paper bags. I didn't much care I had to get regular hepatic tests given that Trileptal could cause liver damage, because the pill allowed me to function normally at least part of the time, without gasping for air at inopportune moments and pulling a lunch sack from my backpack.

Had I recorded my own reggae track during this era, the title would have been "Do Worry". Indeed, I was incorrigibly anxious, even if I fancied myself brave; sometimes I'd hear my mother call me "warrior" when she really said "worrier". But while she lived with us, Dezna soothed me and became my closest childhood friend. She established a nanny state, one of equilibrium. She was a guiding force amid choppy seas – my one true halyard.

Not all mothers are designated as such through genetics or legal parameters. Sometimes someone comes into our life and provides an invaluable maternal influence we hadn't recognised as necessary. The person's nourishment is not simply synthetic Similac but authentic sustenance.

Miss Dezna

I most treasured the breakfast moments we spent over dumpling and tea – jentacular moments, I should say – where Dezna would have me read the newspaper aloud to boost my vocabulary. She perfected my diction and aspired to decorate my speech with "haspirations". As a result, flat vowels, like rock plunks in Caribbean coves, irrigate my voice.

And her calm, contagious as a yawn, hovered over my childhood years like a protective buffer. There were the walks to the bus stop in winter, the bath-time Jamaican bobsled she'd create by cocooning me between two towels, which allowed her to pour into my ears the West Indian time signature, the syntactic steel drum. She was always by my side on wormy mornings – the dawn downpours drawing nightcrawlers from the soil. She guided me, without fail, through wooded trails on honeysuckle afternoons.

Because she arrived when I was just a year and half old, I never knew life without Dezna. And she continued to belay me emotionally throughout my life. But as her sickness worsened, I felt the reliable handhold of my childhood lose its grip and slip away. *Tempus fugit.* As they say about the past, the days are long, the years short.

I wanted to be back with Dezna, blowing the grey fuzzies from dandelions, biting onion grass, chasing newts, breaking wishbones. It was a childhood of skipped rocks across Stony Brook, of counting the seconds between lightning flashes in summer storms. It was fading, disappearing too soon.

She used to talk of her island, of goats baa-ing and sweet Julie mangoes in the morning. "Suppose one day you will visit me there," she would say. It was an enchanting suggestion, but one that always seemed improbable, pure fantasy.

The week after my first visit to Newark, I went back to see Dezna with Tiffan, a blonde actress from Oklahoma I had started dating. She was recently back from touring Asia in *The Sound of Music* and we had met on the Hampton Jitney when she was returning to Manhattan from her stint as a nanny in Quogue. Because I knew we would get married, I had to have Tiffan meet this special woman in my life. But Dezna had moved to hospice by then and did not wake up during our visit. It pained me to stand over my dear nanny's bed, to see her wizened and supported by an IV. It was difficult to say her name and have her not hear – lost in some deep sleep, unable to voice any response with that legato cadence. Tiffan held Dezna's hand and sang gently to her.

A week later, Dezna's daughter Carla called to tell me Dezna had passed. Diabetes, and the attendant heart and kidney problems, dimmed Dezna's vitality until it collapsed and extinguished like the death of a star. Carla, who had visited our house with Dezna when I was in high school and who would go on to sign the ketubah at my wedding (where we served sweating bottles of Red Stripe and I walked down the aisle to Bob Marley's "Is This Love"), provided some simple biographical information when I floated questions about Dezna's life. But when Carla and I reminisced about Dezna at my wedding, I realised just how much I didn't know about my nanny, her past tucked away like a trundle bed.

I always assumed Dezna was from Montego Bay, where she'd go every Christmas. But Carla corrected me and explained about Mahogany Hill, a town in the mountains of St Elizabeth where Dezna was raised. Of course, the revelations continued. Dezna was so pious, so proper and reserved, and spoke only of her husband, George. I surmised he was the father of all her eight children – that is, until I realised her sons, whom I'd later meet for the first time, had different last names. As it turned out, she'd had children by three different men, only the last of whom was her husband. I had only scratched the surface. Now as an adult, I finally began to investigate her arrival to our tony Ivy League community under complex circumstances, quite a different view of the woman who sang me lullabies at bedtime and held a washcloth to my forehead when I was sick.

The adults we idolise and idealise as kids are often history-less in our minds. They are simply sources of comfort and strength. I had but a hazy vision of the true Dezna as the can-do-anything person of my childhood. Her time in Jamaica represented a lacuna in my understanding of her and myself.

So my desire to connect with my nanny in her absence sent me on a dizzying quest to track down her siblings and eight children to uncover the story of Miss Dezna.

But my search, a head-first dive, became a taxing one. That's because there had been a tacit privacy agreement Dezna upheld with my parents during my childhood to maintain order in our house and also obscure the chaos of her own life. Of course, the exchange of information throughout my childhood with

ANOTHER MOTHER

Dezna was asymmetrical. She knew everything about the Urkens – too much, perhaps – and we knew entirely too little about her. My understanding of her life was, at best, a vague approximation, like my conception of Celsius temperatures.

That's because parents apply a don't-ask-don't-tell policy. The terms and conditions are roughly: I trust you, my hired nanny, to give maternal care and even love to my children, but I will not ask, nor do I expect to know, anything about your own family. Another fundamental statute: I realise I am paying you to lavish love and care on my children in place of the time you might spend with your own – I just don't want to hear too much about that sob story. As part of this wilful blindness, the nanny's past is protected from the rest of the household.

Lamenting the fact that there was so much I had yet to learn about the woman who lent me her accent and shaped who I had become, I felt compelled to connect with her family and homeland.

Dezna was more than a Jamaican Mary Poppins, of course. My mission to understand her origins would change our house's conspiracy of silence and lead me on an unorthodox path to learn her story through her kids. Dezna had always been a cipher kept just out of reach. I wanted to decode the past and close that gap.

I plumbed my childhood memories and examined the emotional ballistics of my homelife to make sense of the unknown in my relationship with my nanny. Dezna – like the two hundred thousand Jamaicans who emigrated to the United States from that storied island in the 1980s to find work, commonly as nannies and sometimes nurses – had her own unique narrative that too long went unexamined.

That history is padlocked, baby-gated, relegated to a cedar closet. Pragmatism – schedules, cleanliness – tends to be a priority among parents; the influence and origin of a particular nanny takes a backseat. What happens in Manila in the Philippines, or Port of Spain in Trinidad, or Mahogany Hill typically stays there.

Jamaican nannies, in particular, are an important staple in American society, but less known is the set of economic and political forces on the island that led to this phenomenon.

Of course, I am not the ideal teller of this story. Dezna herself would weave a more poignant narrative about her life, not strained through my lens. But because that is not possible, I am the humble courier of her tale.

4. Mum's the Word

*I*t was reflecting on that care, that mothering, that drove me to try to understand Dezna's origins, and as a professional journalist and wannabe-sleuth, I took a trench coat-detective approach. I scoured historical copies of the *Jamaica Gleaner* newspaper, compiled dossiers from the Jamaica Archives in Spanish Town, and met with some of her family members to gather more biographical details. But everyone agreed, I should focus on talking to Dezna's siblings. Trouble was, of her three living siblings, only two would be of any help, as her brother Frank was suffering a bout of dementia and nearing the end in Jamaica.

"Why you ask *so* many questions?" said Dezna's sister Rohena (aka Aunt Arena), her voice full of gentle reproach – a hearkening back to my childhood. I was talking to her through Google Voice, dialing from Manhattan's Upper West Side down to Kingston through the Magic Jack she uses to communicate with the US. With each syllable, Rohena revived Dezna's essence in that plaintive sing-song.

But this was the third time Rohena had stonewalled me when I gently interrogated her about Dezna. It was difficult to explain inquiries of this kind to a woman in her late 60s set in her ways. Research questions? Reminiscences about episodes decades-old? Those just didn't compute for Rohena. *Why bother?* – she seemed to say. That I was appreciative of her sister made sense. But the extent to which I felt indebted did not translate.

The first time I tracked her down, she was enthusiastic, if bemused, to take my call. Dezna left Princeton on weekends to stay at her house in nearby West Orange and go to church. She'd heard of me over the years and was delighted to learn of the legacy Dezna left on my life. Rohena launched into praise for her sister – her attention to family, her healing prowess, her strength. But in a matter of minutes, she was brusque, bored of answering. She started deflecting my inquiries to other relatives, like Dezna's second oldest son.

"Maybe you ask Orville..." she said, maybe not so coincidentally losing reception.

The next time I tried her, I was impressed by how much could be conveyed in a single hello – perplexed impatience, mostly.

"Mi on mi way to the store," she continued. "Mi gone."

"Mi gone" is pretty definitive in Jamaican parlance in its dismissiveness. It's somewhere between "bye, Felicia" and "smell you later."

I could try her again later if that would be O.K., I said. Maybe she'd be around, she said – non-committal, enjoying the ruse, testing me to see how much I really had invested in talking to her.

ANOTHER MOTHER

For a couple weeks, I'd call – no answer. I tried different times of the day, different numbers I had for her – all to no avail; the phone just kept ringing down there in Kingston resonating through her cozy house of cedar carvings – no answering machine, no Rohena. Then one September evening, I tried her house line, and remarkably, she picked up. The TV whirred in the background, and she had no trouble mentioning to me that her show was on.

I understood I was making a tall order – urging her to think back upon that history, the painful weight of nostalgia. But I was asking about the important old days, Dezna's Jamaica days. I was prepared for her stories of life in the Jamaican hills.

I sat at my kitchen counter on a stool, ready. I listened to her voice through Skull Candy Reggae headphones – red, yellow, and green on the earmuffs. *Hit me with it. Hit me with your memories.*

Then came her favourite phrase: "Why you ask *so* many questions?"

"Maybe we meet one day in person," she said as a valediction.

Suddenly she was talking more and spiritedly so – seeming to continue our conversation. A change of heart?

Turns out she was just yelling at the TV during her show without hanging up; after all, she was Dezna's sister.

Yes, she stymied me three times in a row, and yet, I viewed this as a challenge to get through, to explore the rich past of Dezna's life.

Rohena's reticence was a cultural and generational symptom. She was cagey – distrustful of an outsider and protective of her past, her tales. Jamaicans, in part from the oral tradition of Ghana's Akan people, from whom many descend, have a rich oral storytelling tradition and the gift of gab. But, of course, that's usually only to those within the inner circle. Rohena determined I was not yet ready.

It was the same with Lloyd, Dezna's brother in Toronto, who lives in the heavily West Indian-populated neighbourhood of Scarborough on the city's eastern edge.

The Google Voice dial tone sounded when I rang him up after my failed attempts with Rohena, and as I communicated my reason for calling, I could hear in his listening noises his affectionate familiarity with who I was but also his standoffishness. I explained my interest in Dezna's life and started with a few basic biographical inquiries. He then emitted the sigh of someone listening to a waiter list off the specials.

"Why these questions?" he said. I prodded further, explained my quest to piece together some missing links in Dezna's biography. Surely, he had heard about me.

"Yes, but you are talking about my *sees-ter*." He said it so sincerely, so sweetly. Lloyd allowed little leeway for further questioning and made me feel like I had committed some rake-steppingly awkward twist of reasoning to contact him by phone. When we said our goodbyes, I felt like I'd just had a job interview where the hiring manager told me, "We'll let you know..."

Given some of this resistance, I knew for starters I had to try someone a little more open who still had the memory of the old guard.

That's when I decided to meet Winston, Dezna's oldest son, on a winter's day. I took the bus from Port Authority in New York to Irvington, New Jersey and met him on a pre-arranged corner downtown. I waved at him through the bus window, and when he boarded, I saw him in focus: a wiry man in his late 50s with white scruff, he wore jeans and a rust-coloured hoodie.

"Raaas…" he said as he walked down the aisle. That's all he needed to say; we shook hands and then embraced. He studied me with his wise eyes and provided narrated commentary on the surrounding neighbourhood in the deep, comforting voice of a pilot announcing a destination's weather forecast. I'd be relying on his age – his experience of being raised in large part by his grandparents, Egbert and Beatrice. During our small talk, he jutted his creaky chin out and ground his gold-crowned teeth like just maybe he was unshelling pistachios. When agreeing with a statement, he nodded his head once with the swiftness seen in the downbeat of an ax.

We pulled into the underbelly of the New Jersey Transit bus garage and maintenance centre and sat down in a drab break room drinking Sprite. It was time for some real talk.

"What was Egbert like?" I asked Winston.

Winston descended into deep thought, lost in some foreign land of the past, of an island whose place and time he could never fully resurrect. He itched at his white scruff and used a curled pointer finger to dab twice at his runny nose. His knuckles were dry from the biting cold outside.

Sitting here with Dezna's son on a cold afternoon darkening toward evening called to mind one particular Christmas season with Dezna.

In 1992 when I was six years old, *The Bodyguard*'s release aroused great attention. Everywhere we travelled in the car – the Saab 900 Turbo – Whitney Houston's belt blasted from the sound system, and Dezna in the passenger seat was particularly taken with the music.

Just after Thanksgiving with the American spirit of consumerism in the air and over the radio waves, we wanted to join in the Christmastime cheer, even as Members of the Tribe. So my sister and I piled into the car with Dezna and my mother to see Santa at MarketFair, a mall in Princeton off Route 1 with a teal metal trim on its façade. The car was a nerve-gas bomb of my mother's Chanel No. 5, and she dropped a lipsticked can of Diet Coke into the console, as always — the rear-view mirror permanently set to a position suited for makeup application, not driving. On the highway at dusk, Dezna would say the red taillights ahead, the white headlights of oncoming traffic, and the blue sky just before nightfall constituted an abstract American flag.

Once inside the mall walking along the white tile, we smelled the aromatic soaps and went into Brookstone to sit on massage chairs. Next, we waited in line for Kris Kringle, Dezna always in a long coat and wool scarf.

When we got to the front of the line, my sister refused to sit on Santa's lap, because her Hebrew school teacher had told her it would be a betrayal. Dezna and I laughed with hearty amusement. We were always in cahoots to exploit the peculiarities of our household and mine out the humour. I, by contrast, went up and got my picture with the fat man. He asked

ANOTHER MOTHER

what I wanted. I described the Donatello Teenage Mutant Ninja Turtle action figure with wind-up legs that could swim in the bath. And I also requested happiness for my family, including Dezna – the woman standing right there in the coat.

On holidays, my parents generally gave Dezna a bit of money, but that year, she asked for something else in addition: the soundtrack tape to the *Bodyguard*.

The tracks had been so pervasive and overpowering that season:

But above all this...I wish-a you...lo-uh-uh-uh-uh-ove...

[Drums...]

An D-eye-eee-eye will always love you.

One afternoon the next week, while I was having my Chips Ahoy afterschool snack, my mother came back with the CD she had bought at Sam Goody on Nassau Street.

Dezna was ironing clothes in the kitchen and watching *General Hospital* – I remember the three burn marks on her skin from various cooking and ironing mishaps, the soffits above her head decorated with fake-ivy-stuffed picnic baskets. The room smelled of sprayed starch.

When my mother presented her with the package, Dezna explained that she didn't have a CD player at her sister's house and had asked for the tape. My mother peeled off the plastic shrink wrapping.

"Well, then I'll keep it."

My mother went over to the CD player, placed the CD in the ejected holster, and turned up the stereo.

Ihhhf E-yyyye... shouuuuld stayyy,

I would only be in...

your way-ee-ay-ayyy ...
So I'll go, but I know...
I'll think of you at every step of the way-ee-ay-ay-ayyyy...

Dezna sat quietly, expressionless.

I studied Winston's spry expression there in the NJ Transit cantina. I started with a new approach, a different question to try to see if he could tell me more about Dezna and her parents.

"Well, what did Egbert look like?" I said.

"He looked like you," he said. "A big beard with the red in it. And the white skin."

"White?" I said, almost surprised into a spit-take while drinking my Sprite.

I paused. Dezna's skin was fair on the colour spectrum, but she was a black woman, no doubt. Surely, he didn't mean that her father, his grandfather, was Caucasian.

"He looked like you," Winston said. "That's what mi say to myself when mi first see you."

Dezna's father, it turns out, was a lilywhite man of Scottish ancestry – whiter than my own. Winston was losing patience with my questions; he looked under-slept and yawned.

"If you want to know about mum, you must go there, mon," he said. "Go to Mahogany Hill."

5. *Exodus*

A month after I met Winston in Jersey, I am in flight in Black River, Jamaica – giving my Jewish travelling companions the slip in search of a driver curiously named Dragon to make it to Mahogany Hill. I stand out in all whites like a cricketer, wearing a button-down and pressed slacks, but my footsteps are subtle enough not to draw attention.

Here I am at twenty-eight in Dezna's native land, searching for my nanny's essence, her origin. Language – as a writer, a human being – has best defined who I am, and Dezna is a part of me in that respect. My oral delivery, after all, comes with an imitative exponent: her Jamaican lilt with hollowed-out vowels and consonants as crisp on the teeth as watercress. What had been performative in my childhood has become ingrained, and since Dezna's death five years before, I have tried to find the root of her strong voice to understand my own. But travelling to Jamaica specifically on a pilgrimage to discover my nanny's history would seem a blunt betrayal of my parents' love, not to mention as gratuitously unkosher as a bacon double cheeseburger. So I deluded even my rude bwoy self and concocted a decoy: I signed up for an exploratory mission to document Jamaica's Jewish cemeteries, some of which have a spooky pirate past.

During this undertaking, the putative reason for my trip to Jamaica, I embedded with a group from the non-profit Caribbean Volunteer Expeditions to survey these forlorn graveyards and investigate the Jewmaican Pirates of the Caribbean. At the very least, went my flawed logic, I'd have some opportunity to find shared terrain with my nanny: here was a shoal connecting the two shores of myself, the Jewish and the Jamaican. But something about that prefab strategy didn't feel right. It was a compromise. And that's why – as nice as the Jewish academics, descendants of Sephardic West Indians, and little old ladies were – I had to reject this clinical glance at life here and find an authentic connection to Dezna by heeding Winston's words. As she used to say, "The *'art* wants what the *'art* wants…," her accent blending the sentimental and aesthetic. And that set in motion my covert communiqué with her oldest daughter, Maxine, and the enlistment of Dragon as chauffeur. Of course, I might draw a tongue-lashing from the crew for shirking my duties, but I was after a different kind of secret hidden in the heart of the Caribbean. It would be easier to beg for forgiveness than ask permission.

Suddenly on this sleepy Black River side street, someone calls out to me in a deep bass, startling me just as I'm slinking into my role as guided-tour defector.

"Ross – Rosstaman! Wah *gwaan, mi yute?*"

ANOTHER MOTHER

It's Dragon, a short, middle-aged fellow standing outside a dirt-splattered van parked by the Anglican Parish Church with its mullioned windows. A bald guy in dungarees and a short-sleeved plaid button-down, he's peering at me from over the thin-lensed sunglasses perched on the tip of his nose. He just emanates cool. Stick him in a suit, and he might easily star in a Ciroc ad.

"Wah gwaan?" I say in greeting. His hand is rough as a longshoreman's when I shake it, and I give him a fraternal pat on his bicep. Dragon is just five-two, but he's built as can be from all the construction work he does. There's a whole story, it is said, to how he acquired his moniker, about which the less said, the better.

Maxine and her friend Nadia are in the back seat, and they slide open the door and step out so we can all exchange a tight embrace.

"Mannas, mi bredda," Maxine says as her own hello. Leave it to Dezna's daughter, who considers me her brother as I do her my sister, to greet me with the slang word derived from "manners" – the implication being it's polite to offer a hearty salutation. Dezna was, after all, a stickler for rules.

Max is forty-seven, about the age Dezna was when she came to the States, and has a mother hen disposition. Her hugs are all bosom – her posture bent forward. She clucks any disapproval with a suck of her teeth. In fact, her nickname is Beez, given her queen bee demeanour.

We pile back in the van, and I hop in shotgun.

The choreography of this exodus resembles a coordinated heist – the careful treading, the hushed voices. Then there comes the simple instruction for Dragon: Step on it.

But the car stalls just as the Jewish volunteer group I've escaped turns the corner and approaches from down the street. If the leaders catch me, I'll be guilted into more cemetery fieldwork and have to forgo this side excursion. I suppose I could have simply informed them of my plans, but that would have been a little less exciting.

Max's hair is tied back to allow puzzled disapproval to appear more easily in wrinkles on her forehead. She also speaks almost exclusively in aphorisms, and when Dragon can't get the car started after a couple tries, she starts her lamentation.

"If it's not the button, it's the buttonhole," she sighs. "A dat mi know fi true." Jamaica doesn't always adhere to the "no problem, mon" script resort brochures provide, the very story Dezna sold me through omission during my childhood. Instead, there's this one guarantee: if it's not one thing, it's another. Maxine knows this all too well and rolls her eyes as if to say, "I can't even."

Dragon shuts the vehicle down and vigorously turns the keys in the ignition – this time with success. He shoots me a side-eye of satisfaction.

"Ah suh we dweet," he says, his voice a hickory synth. *That's how we do it.*

Now it's time to *bus'.*

Under the cloak of shade in an alleyway – the stuccoed homes stretch tall to catch whatever breeze possible in this

ANOTHER MOTHER

baking Jamrock January – we beat a path inland toward the hills where the pumpernickel-coloured soil is loamy. There it will be possible to find Dezna's origins, her childhood homestead.

"Don't forget who your real family is," my mother would have said had I informed her of this detour. It's a breach – Benedict Arnoldowitz that I was – of the contract implicit in most childcare situations: the nanny's story outside the house is verboten. No trespassing.

Of course, the agreement works both ways. Dezna, when she moved in with my family in 1988, also supported this emotional Chinese wall. In our house, in her coral-pink carpeted bedroom, where she curled her hair, pulling back her hairline from her forehead, Dezna deflected all personal curiosities. The painful parts of her former life she wanted to forget. And talk of the loved ones she left behind only stoked the embers of longing. Dezna's past, as such, was a fortified city.

With the implementation of this omertà, the parental love was thus secure, supreme, or so my parents hoped. Of course, my father was in slack-jawed awe of the woman who held his family together. My mother certainly felt a combination of envy and gratitude, given Dezna's peaceful approach to problems in contrast to her own overbearing freneticism. Cindy smothered me; Dezna mothered me.

Typically, the nanny's full backstory is extraneous, the wall she puts up to prevent its telling impervious. That is, unless the true turmoil exists in the household, and the nanny, a product of a topsy-turvy environment of her own, turns the tables and provides calm – and not just that, but becomes a boy's safety net, protecting him from anxiety and a potential crack-up.

In that scenario, the childproof, Windexed house is not the sanctuary; the nanny and her native land are. And it's then that you get in the car with Dragon, Maxine, and Nadia and head for the hills. So here I am, maintaining disappearances.

As Dragon guns the engine in Black River toward Dezna's house in Mahogany Hill, I think back to three days earlier: under a slate sky, I am tramping with a dozen others through the high grass of spooky Hunt's Bay Cemetery, a Jewish burial ground located in a shantytown by the Red Stripe factory just outside Kingston. Today, the area is a gang mainstay, and a couple of teenage toughs tell me, as is the Jamaican stereotype, not to worry about a thing. "We're your protection," one says. Past a herd of cattle that white egrets are pecking, the crew and I find what we are looking for: seven gravestones chiselled with Hebrew benedictions and skull-and-crossbones symbols – clues that reveal a peculiar past of cutlass-wielding Semitic corsairs.

Centuries ago, the coffins interred here at Hunt's Bay were ferried from nearby Port Royal, a town on the tip of a narrow peninsula across Cagway Bay from Kingston. Once known as "the wickedest city in the world" and an inspiration for the Pirates of the Caribbean amusement park ride and Hollywood movie franchise, Port Royal was formerly the stomping grounds of Jamaica's little-known Jewish seafaring nogoodniks.

ANOTHER MOTHER

Jews have been part of Jamaican life for some five hundred years, shaping the texture of the island and distilling the quintessence of the country we recognise today. They first arrived in Jamaica in 1494 as part of Columbus's crew, hiding their religious identity as crypto-Jews and fleeing the Spanish Inquisition. Many were successful gold traders and sugar merchants.

Such history gives coincidental context for the common Reggae mondegreen – a mishearing of the opening lyrics to Bob Marley's "Redemption Song" as "old pirates, yes – they rabbi" instead of "old pirates, yes, they rob I" with the Jamaican vocalic alchemy converting o and a into the same sound.

Some Jamaican Jews were marauding privateers, like Moses Cohen Henriques, a crony of Captain Henry Morgan's who once plundered the modern-day equivalent of almost $1 billion from a Spanish galleon in the seventeenth century. The island provided an unlikely haven for religious freedom and a place for Yiddishkeit to thrive in the New World.

In the eighteenth century, Guillaume-Thomas Raynal, a French Enlightenment writer, noted that Jews could adopt Jamaica as a homeland in the Caribbean, given that it was already a Semitic commerce hotbed that would allow them acceptance and safety.

I was also a Jew looking to adopt Jamaica as a sort of homeland for very different reasons.

For their part, Dezna's family members think it's hilarious Jamaica has this underground Semitic history at all. They'd never heard about it until I shared with them the backstory, because today's Jamaican Jewish population consists of fewer than two hundred people. There are, though, at least twenty-one Jewish burial grounds across the island, and that's where this journey is focused: to transcribe epitaphs and compile an inventory of gravesites. The weathered stones slathered in cement are fragile here at Hunt's Bay – with marble veining meeting chipped limestone and remnants of pilfered granite. Amid Hebrew benedictions and the hands of Kohanim (high priests), there are the engraved craniums of Jolly Roger.

Roosters crow on rusty rooftops and palm trees rise into the city's appropriately named Beverly Hills, as volunteers mill with clipboards. Some gravestones are trilingual with Hebrew, English, and also Spanish or Portuguese. Sometimes a volunteer – one of the little old ladies or a bona fide academic – can decipher a carver's inscription if she brushes some baking flour atop. If the stone is still unpronounced, a conservator might wait for the raking light in the late afternoon.

A young girl, no older than seven, wanders into the graveyard with her brother and his friends to investigate the activities of this group that consists mostly of white Americans. She boldly approaches me, noting my poufy hair and then my shaggy beard that from the profile looks like it has been shaded on with a jagged coloured pencil.

"You pritty," she says. "You fazzy."

"*Fuzzy*," her brother corrects her.

"Fazzy," she says, standing on a horizontal gravestone to run her right hand through my hair. I want to explain how my own heritage, unfamiliar to her, had influenced Rasta dreadlocks seen across the island.

ANOTHER MOTHER

After all, Rastafari, one of the most patent features of Jamaican culture, is inextricably linked to Judaism. Haile Selassie, the former Ethiopian Emperor whom Rastas consider to be the messiah, is said to be the direct descendant of the biblical King Solomon and the Queen of Sheba, whose son brought Falasha Judaism to Ethiopia. Rastafari emerged as an Abrahamic religion in 1930s Jamaica with strong connections to Semitic Ethiopia. Dreadlocks are an adherence to a Leviticus commandment not to cut hair and a representation of the Lion of Judah. Rasta culinary strictures, known as *ital*, follow many kosher laws. And Jah, the Rastafarian name for God, comes from Yahweh. And then there's reggae, whose king, Bob Marley, was the son of Captain Norval Marley, himself the son of Jamaican Ellen Broomfield, who was thought to have Jewish Syrian roots.

I strongly identify as Jewish and was amazed to learn about this Jamaican history, but my true Jamaican connection, I felt, was separate from all that. The pirate chronicles struck a chord from an intellectual standpoint but only bolstered my desire to go elsewhere and tackle a more emotional engagement with Dezna.

Across the water from Hunt's Bay, I traipse through Port Royal past homes in bright purples and pinks, past the Tartan and khaki blurs of running children in school uniforms, as I try to track down a cold Ting. This was once a salty pirate hub known for its bordellos, and it's still possible to visit the women's prison, whose purpose was to "allay the furie of those hott Amazons", according to the 1687 account of the naturalist writer John Taylor. Until a 1692 earthquake left it a sunken pirate city, Port Royal was the first true Jewish settlement in Jamaica. Jewish merchants and buccaneers gathered here in 1655, after the British captured Jamaica from the Spanish and Oliver Cromwell allowed for Jewish immigration to England and its colonies.

I smell ganja smoke and burning peat as I wander past Fort Charles, which the British built in the 1650s to secure the entrance to Kingston Harbour against Spanish attacks. I decide to wend my way through the town at dusk toward Gloria's, a beloved local mainstay that serves curried conch, sea eggs, escovitch fish, a seafood-heavy "buccaneer's mix", and fried bammy (Jamaica's traditional cassava flatbread). Under flaxen palm fronds, I wash away the heat with a chilled Red Stripe and look out at Kingston. It takes on a picaroon allure as I gaze across the harbour at it, twinkling in the twilight like doubloons in a treasure chest.

Dragon jerks the van around a jughandle, and Black River fades increasingly into the background. I come to and realise I am charting a more urgent and authentic course here in my connection to the island.

There is an insane method to Jamaican hills driving, one Dragon has mastered. Accelerate fast and without fear around blind turns. Just start beeping right before you turn the wheel around a hairpin. It becomes a dangerous game of chicken when another car is taking the curve from the opposite direction, and the drivers work on fleet-footed instinct to avoid disaster. Never mind the gully waiting to receive the van in a flaming ball of death: the tyres have proper traction treads, supposedly, and Dragon has a sixth sense for the width of the roadway.

Jamaica continues British motorway customs and traffic laws, and Dragon notices my discomfort as he red-lines.

"The left side is the right side, and the right side is suicide," he says, as if that will put me at ease while he vrooms up the escarpment and fishtails around a boulder.

As far as I see it, left and right both fall into the latter category as the brakes wheeze. Throughout my whole life when I'm feeling jittery before a flight or in a situation I deem dangerous, I recite the Hebrew *shema* prayer to myself. Short and direct to the source, it efficiently accomplishes the little bit of protection I'm seeking. Still, I'm white-knuckling the whole way.

To minimise my anxiety, I try to make small talk with Dragon. I ask him about his family, how many kids he has. He takes his left hand off the wheel and puts up his pointer finger to indicate one, then lets the rest of the fingers on his hand trickle with spirit fingers indicating some creative arithmetic: the answer is unquantifiable. He throws his head back and laughs.

In St Elizabeth, we drive past YS Falls, a series of seven cascades, and dog-leg left up an unmarked, unpaved road – the citrus light streaking in the windows in sun spots under the custard sky. Wispy cotton-ball clouds hang over the crumpled mountains, creating dark oval shadows on the hillsides.

Dragon calls out to all his ladies through the mini villages with low-slung houses neatly arranged among heaths.

Yeah, yeah, yeah, yeah.

That's his typical salutation. It may seem lackadaisical or rude to the uninitiated, but it's a hearty greeting on the island.

"Why you nuh answer my calls?" Dragon screams out at a nicely dressed lady waiting for the hill tram.

"You nuh *cyaaall* me," the woman replies.

Dragon lets forth a maniacal laugh and keeps driving.

I shoot Maxine a look in the backseat to gauge her reaction. She rolls her eyes at Dragon's antics. Nadia makes her right hand a fin and puts it up to her forehead like a visor – shielding her eyes in embarrassment.

Yeah, yeah, yeah, yeah, he goes, all the way up the hill.

As we bounce under the welter of the unpaved roads in this suicide vehicle, we wind our way up a mountain overlooking lush green pineapple groves and eventually pull off to the side of the road: there in Mahogany Hill is Old McDonald Farm, a smattering of land enveloping a modest structure with clapboard siding and a rivulated zinc roof. The hinges along the windows and doors are verdigris from years of rain. Blooming poui trees explode in pinks and yellows. Next to the house is a guango tree, which Jamaicans call a "story tree". They're hundreds of years old and have many of their own tales to tell. Here we are in Dezna's *selva selvaggia* on a day hot as a beagle's breath. The humidity creates a lather on my face, and I feel an atmospheric pressure drop as if a storm's approaching.

Here we are in "country", as Jamaicans say. Our little crew steps out of Dragon's van and approaches the house, the yolky sun over easy in a cloud. This is Dezna's past, emerging from the overgrowth like a lost city.

ANOTHER MOTHER

I peer up at the A-frame truss, then over at the porch, and sigh, wondering what life must have been like here, what stories have occurred within these walls. What would it be like to live here so far from what I'm used to?

This nog-walled ramshackle structure, one of the finest here, was once, I would learn, the scene of so much laughter and heartbreak.

Out come Dezna's nephew Junior and his wife, Queen, the current residents of the McDonald Farm. Junior, bearded and wearing a Red Stripe shirt over his gut, smokes a fat blunt and gives me a bear hug. He's overflowing with bonhomie, partly attributable to his indulgent puffs of jazz lettuce.

"Mannas," he says, leaning on a moringa tree. "Erryting criss?" He uses "criss", a patois word meaning "all right", with an amused lift to his brow – half testing my vocabulary, half accepting me as a family insider.

"Respek," I say. "Erryting criss."

Queen, in a white skirt and with her hair tied back in a navy bandana, is entertained by our banter, and she steps away from her zungu pan to make eyes at her husband and assess whether my language is authentic enough to earn me, even if jokingly, the country's demonym.

"Him real Yardie," she says. "Nuh true?"

"A mi fi tell you," Junior says in agreement. *I'm telling you...*

Maxine, Nadia, and I are viewed as fresh workers and asked to pick gungo peas for the shipment to town Junior needs to make.

"After, you have a jelly," Junior says, referring to freshly cracked coconut that gets its name from the tapioca-textured flesh inside. He also whispers he has some steel bottom (Jamaican moonshine) that he can pour into a serious batch of kick-down (local rum punch). In a pantomime, he exaggerates the act of swallowing with his Adam's apple lifting and dropping in a cartoonish glug-glug. He smiles slyly and puffs on his skunky spliff.

In the bushes Dezna played in as a child by a guango tree, I press my fingertips to remove the gungo peapods from the stems and place them in a wooden basket. I am labouring on Dezna's land, and my thoughts turn to our walks together in the woods by Hale Drive in Princeton, my hand in hers. Time slows down here: in these fields, it is possible to notice the way a droplet of dew elongates before it falls from a leaf, the trees softly soughing.

Ubiquitous here – the laughter of nanny goats and stench of noni fruit, a berry that feels like a moist eyeball plucked from an obeah man and stinks like toenail fungus cheese. Peeny-wallies, Jamaican flying click beetles, soar around the bushes filled with violet agapanthus flowers. Doctor birds, the streamer-tail hummingbirds, flit from one sugary bush to the next in this sylvan paradise.

Dragon scales the trunk of a tree with a machete in hand and chops down some coconut for us to drink and then consume. As we eat, the silence is sacrosanct.

In this quiet moment, I try to imagine Dezna in these fields, in this house. In my mind, she is sitting on the veranda and bursting into one of her fits of laugher that requires her to catch her breath.

ANOTHER MOTHER

Of course, it will take many conversations, meals, walks, and visits with her children and the people of these hills, the ones who recall Miss Dezna, to find her true story.

6. *Thanks and Praise*

*D*ezna has off. Dezna is coming.

I am twenty-two and have been so busy that recently I've only talked to my nanny occasionally by phone. But it's Thanksgiving, and she'll be joining us at the vinyl-sided townhouse at the edge of Princeton, the one my mom moved into after my parents divorced.

My parents, who have been apart for five years, are now dating each other again. And Dezna will find herself in a peculiar new environment when she reencounters the family she so long looked after. Princeton revisited.

It happened by chance. I'd called Dezna on her birthday, November 10, and realised we were overdue for a get-together. Without consulting anyone, I'd extended an invitation.

In my family, everyone knows my bond with Dezna is special, so I am tasked with fetching her from the train station. Dezna is in a top coat and red beret when she walks out of the Dinky onto the platform. I get out of the car and hug her – the smell of her castor oil, her warm hug are familiar sources of comfort. She holds my shoulders and looks at me.

"Still getting taller, Ras-mon," she says, with an umhmm-umhmm mutter of approval.

I open the passenger-side door for her and set off, farther than usual in Princeton, to the new house. We drive along the familiar roads, past the colonial houses and neo-Gothic spires rising above the treetops towards the sky – the smell of burning chimneys over the borough and the squawks of birds heading south for the winter. Though I don't yet know it, this is the last time I will see Dezna before that hospital visit in Newark. We have entered stoppage time.

My mother's new bestie, a divorcée who teaches spin class and had brought along her new talking-haircut of a boyfriend to the house, has left after spending most of the early afternoon with us (Linda, after hearing of our former nanny: "I don't know if I could handle a celebrity in our midst."), so Dezna and I enter the aubergine foyer to relative quiet when we arrive.

I hang her coat and hat in the closet and notice her hair is a bit greyer, with a smokiness to it at the roots.

Nicole comes downstairs.

"Dez-naaaaa…"

Dezna beams. She has an ability I've never quite encountered in anyone else – to project joy without moving a single facial muscle. She seems to emit light from her eyes, her cheeks.

They hug.

"Put on a little weight," Dezna mutters in a cutely squeaked tone under her breath.

"What?" Nicole challenges. "Dezna, *what?*"

Dezna and I smile at each other, that complicit smirk we've always shared. She doesn't mean the comment in any malicious way. This is just her way of reintegrating into the house, noting anything new. Nicole stands arms akimbo in amused shock.

"Dezna!" my dad says, entering from the living room. This mini reunion is like one of veterans reconvening years after battle – recalling the trenches of Hale Drive. My dad acts as if he's approaching a Purple Heart honouree. He hugs her and stands back, shifting from side to side as if settling into a golf stance.

"How you been?"

"Everything all right, Irv."

My mother, on cue, walks in from the kitchen, chewing a Triscuit with chopped liver spread on it.

"Oh, Dezna..." she says, smacking her lips and testing the elasticity of her nose's underside with the bent knuckle of her pointer. "I'm glad you're here...I need to ask you about the turkey."

Dezna smiles, and I bug my eyes out at her and halt for a moment as if to say: *nothing's changed.*

"Yes, Cindy," Dezna says. "Let me see..."

"Hiya, hi!" my mother says, catching herself and backtracking to the pleasantries of a greeting. She rubs Dezna's shoulder as she gets close. "What's doin'? Nice to have you here."

"Yes, Cindy..."

My two mothers, the citrus and nightshade queens, disappear into the kitchen, where the oven fan is blasting.

ANOTHER MOTHER

The afternoon is a blur, as happens with an event whose importance you don't take stock of as it's unfolding. We never know when will be the last time we'll have the opportunity to interact with someone at length, when we'll have the chance to show appreciation. Had I realised this was to be our final true time together, I would have hugged Dezna more closely. I would have actively asked everything I could about her life and her history. I would have poured her some rum. Of course, it is impossible to Ctrl+Z the past.

At that time, I am trying to be a writer and have adopted the look of tousled troubadour. I am living in Brooklyn. I am selling articles. I am tutoring for a wealthy Jamaican family in Fort Greene. Dezna says to be careful in Brooklyn. I am trying to get my life together. I am eating jerk chicken at The Islands in Crown Heights. After two internships at prestigious publications, I am figuring things out. I am a bit adrift post-college, a meanderthal, thinking of moving to Berlin, where rents are cheap and the avant-garde is alive and well. I am trying to make something of myself worthy of Dezna's rearing. These are years of pluck and striving. I am trying to be a man of letters. Licence to quill. *(I know, I know . . . I am becoming my father.)* But the reaching out to Dezna gets lost in the shuffle; life gets in the way of life. She is working elsewhere, and I am studying. And growing into myself. The full sails of our relationship begin to luff. That Thanksgiving it had been almost as many years since she left our house as she had spent with our family. The empty years are wrapped up in a strange rotating vortex of time.

There are the inevitable woulda-couldas of that afternoon: I would have uttered so many more I-love-yous and thank-you-Deznas for instilling in me a passion for language, a curiosity about the world. For a woman who provided such unconditional love, I find in reflecting upon this afternoon together that I use the conditional tense tensely.

As we knife brie cheese onto crackers, Dezna shows me pictures of the little girl and boy she watches from the family she went to care for after we grew up. She tells us, in the hushed cushiness of her voice, how smart they are.

I wish I could have sat with Dezna and talked adult-to-adult and wrung out the past I didn't understand. Instead, I am putting casseroles on the table, green beans with crispy onions and sweet potatoes stuck with marshmallows, and ramekins of sauces. And my mother is going about her usual talking points.

"Dezna...," my mother starts to say, and Dezna mutters dismissively. She has an uncanny ability to anticipate based on verbal tones how a sentence will go – like audience applause after the first strummed bar of a hit. Dezna takes conversation on the volley, not the groundstroke. "Dezna, don't you think *Roo-aws* needs a haircut," my mom says. "Tell him. Dezna, are you listening?"

In this carved-out development at the edge of Princeton, with rolling hills and a half-decent pool, we are reunited. A family once more, altered.

In replaying this afternoon over in my mind, I feel a heaviness in my chest.

ANOTHER MOTHER

The people who enter into our lives unannounced of unclear origins who stay and linger, we all too often don't ask the necessary questions about them. For so long the shade has stayed and shrouded truth, and we somehow have not illuminated the mysteries. We accept this blindfold as status quo. Meaningful figures are mere silhouettes. But suddenly, at some point after the person's left us, we want the truth. By the following Thanksgiving, Dezna will be in the hospital in Newark, then on her deathbed in hospice. Maybe I can only live with Dezna through my eidetic memory, I think. I am trying to trigger synapses, take journeys in my mind – walks to the bus stop, games of Guess Who? and Sorry! and the Original Memory Game.

After the Urken Thanksgiving meal, during which we all go around with raised glasses of grape juice saying what we're thankful for (that Dezna has joined us seems to be the theme), the shadowy corners of the house darken as the afternoon moves toward dusk. Dezna will go back soon.

"Dezna, I want to show you something," I say. "I've been writing about you." I explain the constant inquiries about the peculiar riddim of my speech and how I've tried to reflect on her true influence.

We trudge up to the room I was assigned in this new house amid that new carpet smell, and I boot up the old Dell desktop as a sash of sunlight cinches the room.

I read to Dezna from the Word document I've been drafting out, just like old times – sounding out syllables for her "loud and proud" – in my bizarro accent that lands somewhere between

Kennedy plummy and dance-hall braggadocio. This fragment of writing is a tribute to her, to her nectar voice, its influence on my own polyphony, my bilingual soul. I languish in the squished kiss of her language. We are here in this carved-out subdivision near the Princeton Tow Path, transplanted across town and time. But the act is the same as when we *read pon di cawna* with chapter books.

I breeze through a couple sentences, and Dezna gets misty-eyed. I am describing her lyceum of life that I attended as a humble cadet, how each micro action she imbued with such love. I read some more, her language on my tongue like the burn of a Scotch bonnet, and she tucks a scrunched-up index finger to the corner of her eyes to catch a tear. Dezna is not one for outward emotions, but I am praising her for all the love she's invested. It is inadequate as a gesture, but I am at least able to provide in this written equivalent of a doodle, a wireframe, the plinth of a monument dedicated to her. There in that room, more than two decades since we had first met, as I grew taller and she got slightly shorter, we have just a moment of togetherness as we hurtle toward an uncertain future. I am no longer that little princeling of Princeton, but Dezna is still a guiding force for me to follow throughout my life. There I am ever so briefly sharing this scribbled appreciation. I have unfinished work to tend to. We are in this temporary house, in this nether-sphere of life – I am just embarking upon my adulthood, and Dezna, though we don't know it, is nearing the end – as my voice ricochets off the peach-coloured Sheetrock walls. Her chewably sibilant syllables that day – I can still hear them like the rustle of leaves outside as the world orbits toward winter.

I needed to gather up the mysterious embers of our past and make sense of them, triangulate truths, convert those smudges into ink. Those unknown moments of her life, I wanted to articulate and order and honour. The feeling of Dezna's absence in my life has been jarring, like the echo in a freshly empty room.

I'd suffer the burdens of medium-rare sleep as this desire to resuscitate her in my mind increased. I wanted to provide testimony to her blessed memory. I have shed too many tears and cried the cries where you can smell the boogers in your nose. I longed for the world she was not long for. My universe is keyed to her sing-song. What's depleted must be replenished. So this is my humble recompense.

This is not a dirge, though. Nor is it an elegy, hagiography, or paean. More precisely, it's a lullaby, to put Dezna properly and sweetly to rest.

Dezna, you are the wave through the bus window, the hand on my forehead, the warm dumpling in my belly, the squealed laughter in the backyard amid Bradford pear trees. You are the excitement of TV's 'You-could-win-a-brand-new-car', the ginger-beer fizziness in my nose, too. You are the Caribbean waterfall at bath time and the whistling kettle spouting steam thick as seafoam. You are the snugness of socks on feet and the thermometer under my tongue. You are the unfurled curls of a scissored ribbon, the smell of sandalwood and castor oil, the morning clang of a teaspoon against the lip of a mug. Time goes always onward, though – somehow.

I would recommend hugging those dear to you more. I would recommend saying, "I love you."

It is the regret of what I didn't say that Thanksgiving Day, of not reaching out as much as I should have that last year of Dezna's life, that galvanised my search into her past. This was not some sentimental journey. It was a true emotional reckoning and inquest into this beautiful woman's history to appreciate her triumphs and sorrows and reconnect with her offspring, who all had special elements of her. My curiosity served as a fillip to set me on this path. And the emotional Kevlar with which she equipped me provided adequate protection to take the bullets of hard truth. I wanted to understand fully the village on the hill where it is possible to locate the reliquary of her essence. I needed to wander the catacombs of her past.

7. Nanny of the Maroons

At the house in Mahogany Hill, Maxine looks up at a tree and spies a plump breadfruit – the rind a green turning towards yellow that I can barely even make out.

"It's a shame," Max says. "It will fall tomorrow."

This knowledge of nature reminded me of Dezna. My childhood with her was about tracking inchworms scroonching through tall grass, finding daddy longlegs in basement corners. We noticed gossamer spidery webs sparkling, and Dezna would communicate with birds who would fly onto the back of her hand.

Suddenly here in Mahogany Hill, a little girl in the street runs by, chasing after her goat – the leash dragging in the dirt.

Dragon scales a banana tree with his machete and starts hacking away at the fibrous purple veins holding a bunch.

Maxine, Nadia, Dragon, and I sit down on some tufted zoysia grass to relax.

Nadia picks at her elaborate maroon braids and sighs in the heat, giving Maxine a gentle nudge. In their Montego Bay neighbourhood of Bogue Village, a community started as a low-income settlement that has evolved into a thriving family enclave just outside the North Coast resort hub, they'll lounge on Maxine's front patio and eat jackfruit as they gossip in rapid patois. Nadia has twin girls who are seven, a grown son ("Mi can't believe mi have *pickney* 'bout to graduate college," she often says), and a world-weariness about her. She is also one of the most passionate Jamaican evangelists I've encountered, and she wonders aloud when I'm going to go to Arlene, her hair girl, to get braids and asks what new patois expressions I've picked up.

"When you come inna Jamrock, chat like a Yardie," she says.

"A mi fi tell you," Dragon says.

Nadia tells me I'm excused for not having sufficient exposure to patois given the exorbitant cost of Jamaican food she experienced during her last trip to New York.

"Sixteen dollars for an oxtail — and *no* rice and peas?" She shakes her head as if some great offence has been perpetrated against her.

But Maxine isn't going to let me get off so easily.

"Man 'pred 'im bed – 'im haffi lidung inna it," Maxine says. I have to lie down in the bed I've made for myself, she means. In my quest for an authentic connection, I've got to walk the walk but also talk the talk.

In Maxine's intonations, her expressions, the crispness of her ds and ts ticking in tandem, I can hear Dezna. Dezna's essence is present here in her birthplace, and I tell Max as much.

"Well, tell me what you remember about Mum," Maxine says.

So I start with one little story.

***

"Write your name," Dezna told me.

I was in preschool and on a playdate at my house with a boy named Benji. We wanted to play Duck Hunt on Nintendo or run around the backyard, but Dezna demanded some degree of discipline. Before you could have fun, you had to complete a serious task. In a playroom that served mostly as the art studio for my frighteningly abstract oil pastel works and installation projects – a lot of Elmer's Glitter Glue and doom – there was a large easel, on which Dezna had my sister writing sentences and trying her hand at spelling words.

"Come on, Maas Ras," she said. "Write your name."

Dezna implored me to start with the capital R – big and strong. She stressed the importance of a strong educational foundation, of eloquence. She sang her common ditty:

> *Good better best*
> *Never let it rest*
> *'Til your good becomes your better*
> *And your better becomes your best.*

Usually obedient, I tried to impress my friend with rebellion. After all, his father was a doctor of some local note, his mother a Swiss scientist with intimidating pince-nez.

We were more interested in armpit farts and scampered away into the adjacent kitchen. Soon, we hatched a plan by the windows there – shielded from the forsythia outside by beige Hunter Douglas venetian blinds beneath a fuchsia blouson valance (my mother had made her design decisions at Urken's in the early '80s, mind you). In the flower beds by the window surrounding the back patio, there are cleomes and impatiens. My father, though, always insisted he grew nothing in his garden but tired.

A confession: there are words I have always had trouble spelling: cemetary, tommorow, comitment.

It is a point of personal shame that even though my nanny spent so much time impressing upon me the importance of developing a command of language at the easel and elsewhere, I still falter at the most basic building blocks of orthography. I have two theories as to why. In those particular words, it could be my aversion to those concepts, respectively: the crushing finality, the uncertain future, the promised concreteness. Another plausible explanation is my exposure to a fluid language growing up. Because my mother tongue itself is in flux – the Jamaican patois seeping into the Mid-Atlantic adagio – language is amorphous for me, a shifting extension of my identity. In *Wheel of Fortune*, Dezna always searched for the right glyphs, mentally manipulated scrambled possibilities. As a result, I'm overstimulated by anagrams, delight in oonerspisms, embrace a personal heteroglossia.

But the duality of my language may also be something of a survival mechanism. In a similar way, I'm ambidextrous.

Though I write, eat, and brush my teeth with my left hand, I do certain activities with my right (despite my once fractured wrist): serving in tennis (though I play left-handed), throwing a baseball, and cutting with scissors (not that I was ever much good at staying in the lines). I have found some tasks and skills easier with a particular side of my body. And given my bifurcated upbringing – Jewish and Jamaican – I am similarly able to rely on advantages in each to approach a certain challenge. That twin sensibility has helped me adapt and persevere when my genetic tendency veers towards anxiety. My Jamaican association has enriched my emotional war chest, supplied a whetstone on which to sharpen my resilience.

Of course, on that day as a child with Benji, my linguistic interests took a backseat to general ragamuffinry. Soon thereafter, we came running back to the playroom, turned around, and wiggled butt. We were rude. We were crude. We were four years old.

Dezna hid her laughter, scrunched up her nose in disgust (her lips raised to her nostrils), and demanded that we obey her. We were to take the Magic Marker and write on the newsprint pad clipped to the easel.

"Come on, a big B and a big R," she said.

Words had power, she told me. They could twist without notice: words become swords.

Instead, we shook some more.

"*Rudie, rudie, rudie come from jail...,*" she sang, as her cheeks lowered into a glower.

And then there came the ultimate shame-inducing blow: "What-a joke to you is death to me," she said.

That's when I knew things got real. We bolted out and through the kitchen and into the dining room to hide behind a credenza.

Once Benji left, Dezna pulled me aside and expressed her disappointment that I had been disrespectful in front of my friend. I looked up at her face, at her cheekbones, her nose wrinkled in disappointment.

I slinked up to my room, and there, knock-kneed on my knock-off Eames chair, fell into an amorphous wad of emotion. I wailed, filled with guilt for betraying this woman who so cared for me.

When I finish my story, Maxine tightens her arm around me in a side hug. I apologise for perhaps going on too long. No, no, Maxine says. These woods, these hills have encouraged tales. This is, after all, how Dezna spent much of her youth. The sky starts to wring out the day's humidity in an afternoon shower, typical of the subtropics – with just the initial slurs of a thunderstorm – and we move a pitching wedge's distance from where we are sitting to the veranda. Raindrops plink on the zinc roof.

It is here, I learn, that Dezna began to love narrative.

***

As evening falls, they gather round the dutch pot there – neighbours trudging from the gully side to congregate at the McDonald farmhouse, the modest structure with clapboard siding and a rinky-dink roof, the nicest in the village. There, high above Holland Bamboo and beyond the alluring waft of the Appleton Estate Jamaica Rum distillery amid acres of sugarcane, sits the modest smattering of humanity called Mahogany Hill.

Egbert McDonald, a carpenter and bauxite miner, overlooks his domain from the porch – lush pineapple groves all around here in St Elizabeth, the "bread basket" of Jamaica, full of fertile land and abundant boscage. He sits, as always, on the cedar throne he carved – his beard exaggerating its red tint in the embers of the early-evening sun. A white man of Scottish descent, he decamped here from nearby Pisgah after his family cut him off once he eloped with Beatrice, a beautiful woman of Maroon heritage and a descendant of slaves. *What a scandal*, his parents thought. *Our son, married to a girl whose ancestors worked on a sugarcane plantation?*

Beatrice tends to the curry goat in the dutchie. Behind her sister Pearl, Dezna is the second-oldest of five and takes on household responsibilities early on for her younger siblings, Lloyd, Frank, and Rohena. Almost ten years old, Dezna has jutting Maroon cheekbones and a shy disposition. She bunches up her cotton frock – with felt patterns she's sewed on herself – and sits down cross-legged. She makes sure Rohena isn't being fussy.

1951, and Jamaica is quiet. 1951, and Jamaica is protected under British rule. 1951, and sugar is abundant. 1951, and in Jamaica, you really don't worry about a thing.

Maas Seamon, that's how Egbert is known. He's a pastor, a farmer, a miner, a yeoman, an everyman. He's planted cedar trees in his yard, the kind you let grow throughout your life and chop down for a coffin to use at your death. The neighbours from the whole of Mahogany Hill congregate around the veranda for storytelling.

It's Saturday, September 1, 1951, and Dezna sits by the hearth on the wood floor with her tea. Pervasive – the stench of noni fruit. Egbert, a magisterial presence, commands attention and prepares to tell a tale, an old legend from this part of Jamaica about Lovers' Leap.

Obsessed with narratives, Egbert's intrigued, in particular, by alterations in fate, how minuscule factors can contribute to a radical plot shift. For example, always a fast runner, he often thinks back to September 27, 1927, when his speed wasn't sufficient; his friend William Cathrick and he were arraigned on a larceny charge after they were caught stealing five goats belonging to Hugh Spencer, overseer at the Midgeham Estate near Savanna-la-Mar. Though Cathrick fessed up and was sentenced to 25 weeks of hard labour in Spanish Town (His Honour Lieut. Colonel C.M. Ogilvie, Resident Magistrate, told Cathrick, "It is one of the most disgraceful things to take away people's horn stock…"), Egbert pled not guilty and made bail in the sum of five pounds. He was, quite remarkably and due to a lack of jurisprudential competence, let off but forced to endure widespread teasing for his peccadillo. One local boy in particular, Wilbert Moncrieffe, gave him hell – disparaging his decision-making skills and brandishing a rare form of

ANOTHER MOTHER

Schadenfreude at Egbert's public embarrassment. As a form of self-flagellation and motivation for not being fast enough, Egbert ran the hills of St Elizabeth, calloused his feet with training up by YS Falls and over to Black River. Cue May 25, 1929, Empire Day – his last year of education at Guy's Hill school. After the schoolchildren sang "Flag of Britain" to wish His Majesty the King a speedy recovery from a recent illness, Egbert dominated in the flat race – edging out none other than Wilbert Moncrieffe from Mount Nebo School. The best stories, Egbert thinks, are redemption stories.

A master raconteur, Egbert steeples his hands to his chin in Mahogany Hill as he lets his modest audience take in the beginning of his story next to the guango tree. Egbert speaks with a relaxed tone as if he's stepping into a warm bath. The neighbourhood's in need of a narrative escape. A week or so back, on August 22, a hurricane blew down twelve houses. The road between Pisgah and Ginger Hill is still blocked.

The northern extremities of St Elizabeth, he tells his captive public, are rangy, with the Nassau Mountains stretching across the northeast, the scoriae of the Lacovia farther west. The Santa Cruz farther south in the parish divide a wide plain, and they stop suddenly in the form of a precipitous sixteen hundred-foot drop called Lovers' Leap.

This is the spot, legend has it, where two eighteenth-century slaves, youthful lovers, jumped to their deaths rather than live life apart. Mizzy and Tunkey fell in love at the Yardley Chase cotton and coffee plantation, but Richard Chardley, their master, took a shine to the beautiful Mizzy. Determined to have her for himself, he arranged to end the slaves' romance by sending Tunkey off to a different estate. In an act of desperation and courage, the lovers fled to start a new future together. But Chardley and his faithful retinue chased them through the Santa Cruz Mountains, Egbert says. Their hearts pounding, their lungs desperate for breath, Mizzy and Tunkey came to the mountain edge, stray rocks dropping into oblivion as they pulled up and shuffled to a stop. The southern edge of Jamaica loomed as they peered over into the Caribbean – Rocky Point, Clarendon to the east and Treasure Beach to the west. They glanced back and saw Chardley fast approaching, his face red with rage. They turned forward and looked down over the drop-off into Cutlass Bay, glinting in moonlight. Instead of being seized and separated, they held each other in a tight embrace and jumped off the cliff towards the annular atolls below.

As Egbert tells the tale, Dezna allows a smile to spread across her lips. She wants love like that – can't-live-without-you love, jump-off-a-cliff-for-you love. A girl from the hills of St Elizabeth can dream of passion.

Egbert pauses and introduces a wrinkle to the tale, as Dezna's eyes begin to close. By the Santa Cruz Mountains, a bystander, an old crone, insisted the lovers did not perish. They avoided the harsh impact of the rocks rising from the sea, because on their descent, the moon caught them in a shining silver net and guided them down gently to safety on the southern shores of Jamaica.

ANOTHER MOTHER

As the adults gathered, sip on sweet rum and nibble at bammy, the starch helping to absorb the high-proof jolt, Egbert begins another story, his favourite.

"Now, now, now, now," he says, rousing the sleepy crowd to attention with his Scottish brogue.

Nanny of the Maroons (aka Granny Nanny) served as a princess chieftainess during the eighteenth century, he says. She led the Maroons, comprised of free black warrior-communities with ties to the Ashanti of Ghana, who left behind life on sugar plantations and successfully resisted British rule. Historical documents have lent credence to her accomplishments, though Jamaica's official archives only make scant mention of her, chronicling her four times.

Nanny, as Egbert tells it, was born to royalty in Ghana and sold into slavery to toil in Jamaica's St Thomas cutting cane. With allies Accompong, Cudjoe, Johnny, and Quao, she escaped and set up a makeshift society in the Blue and John Crow Mountains, where she brought fear to the British army, the strongest in the world.

Nanny and her cohort thrived by avoiding detection, pioneering the jerk method of cooking in pit fires so as not to draw attention from the British army. Nanny is mytho-poetic; she is said to have been an obeah woman, practising magic and sorcery. When British soldiers shot their guns at her army, Egbert said, she caught the bullets with her butt cheeks and refired the rounds back at the Brits.

"Straight from her batty," Egbert says.

Even exaggeration indicates some element of near truth in Jamrock. Jamaicans, as Egbert tells it, explain that truth in an axiom: *"If it nuh go so, it go near so."*

Along with her warriors, Nanny would dress up as a tree, covering herself with leaves and branches. Using necromancy, she'd draw groups of soldiers near and ambush them, killing them one by one. Of course, the Maroons would spare one single soldier so that he would go back to a commander and report that the trees had come alive and lay waste to his garrison; the soldier, in turn, would be institutionalised under suspicion of mental illness.

The crowd hoots as Egbert tells the tale.

Next, he explains how Granny Nanny became legendary for her healing powers, learned as she was in herbal methods. She treated her soldiers who were wounded or overcome with sickness, making the concoctions of kabba kabba and lemongrass, for instance. Dezna listens to the various potions and remedies Nanny concocted, imagining the potential powers of the Maroons, her mother's ancestors. Dezna wants to be Nanny, an obeah woman.

As the tale ends, Dezna is sleepy, having spent all day harvesting in the ginger grove and picking hogberry and jimbilin.

The fires that have licked their tongues into the night die down, and Beatrice throws sand on the last embers as only the Pleiades shine from above. Dezna says this is paradise – the end-of-day tea served, the soporific storytelling. Dezna is almost

ANOTHER MOTHER

ten years old. Just a girl in the hills of St Elizabeth, Jamaica. At bedtime.

Beatrice gathers by her five children and sings Jamaican work songs from the plantations as lullabies. And then she always ends with "Linstead Market":

> Carry mi ackee go a Linstead Market
> Not a quattie wut sell
> Carry mi ackee go a Linstead Market
> Not a quattie wut sell
>
> Lawd! What a night, not a bite
> What a Satiday night
> Lawd! What a night not a bite
> What a Satiday night
>
> All di pickney dem a linga, linga
> Fi wha dem mumma no bring
> All di pickney dem a linga, linga
> Fi wha dem mumma no bring
>
> Lawd! What a night, not a bite
> What a Satiday night
> Lawd! What a night, not a bite
> What a Satiday night.

Dezna drifts off to sleep.

8. *Could You Be Loved?*

When I meet Winston after my return from Mahogany Hill at the house of Fabi, Dezna's youngest daughter (her washbelly, as is said), I have gained some considerable street cred. In describing the details of my visit to Mahogany Hill – the gungo pea bushes, the noni fruit, my time with Junior and Dragon – I legitimise myself to him.

"Well, well, well," he says, sizing me up, a mere padawan to his jedi. He's rocking a faded red hoodie and navy sweatpants and has the Dezna glint in his eye – ever game, if slightly bashful. He strokes his chin in thought and ovals his mouth as if preparing for a close shave. "Junior, him a rudebwoy," Winston says, hack-laughing.

As close as I felt to Dezna in seeing the house where she grew up – a reverse journey of her arrival to our house in Princeton to become part of our family – I couldn't help but feel unsatisfied. I'd had just a taste of Dezna's environment and what life was like for her growing up in the 1940s and 1950s in the hills of St Elizabeth. I'd seen her origins and wanted to try to put more parts of the puzzle together about what shaped her and what she experienced in her life. What were jukes and pivots of Jamaica's own development and how would they eventually influence Dezna's life?

That meant trying to learn about the next stage of her life with a man whose name I did not know and who, until recently, I didn't even realise was part of the equation.

In some ways, I felt protective of Dezna. Some man, Winston's father, had apparently done Dezna wrong, and I wanted to comprehend that strife, curse that man for his disregard.

I became cognizant of the fact that I had always wanted to defend Dezna, because I had an understanding from an early age of what she meant to me as a second mother – one I didn't necessarily deserve but one who proved, in many ways, so necessary.

Once during a family gathering at our house in Princeton when I was four, my grandfather, the tomato magnate, was demanding service. He needed another Coke and wanted assistance from the kitchen while we sat in the dining room.

"Dezma," he said, mispronouncing her name, perhaps purposely – laughing. "Dez-*ma*!" To him she was a mere domestic worker.

My parents sat in silence.

"Dez-*ma*?!" he said.

"Pa," I said. "Her name is Dez*na*."

He looked at me with shock, and Dezna squint-smiled as she brought the soda over.

Given Dezna's caretaking role in our house, I always viewed her in my childhood as a pure source of maternal comfort – middle-aged and ever-wise. But sitting here with Winston and delving into how Dezna was a vibrant young woman who attracted much attention in the village with her balletic movements, I had an entirely new perspective on my nanny. Seeing Dezna as a beautiful romantic being became a paradigm shift for me.

The details I eventually discovered would pain me as I inspected her biographical forensics. Of course, I didn't expect all of Dezna's past to be hunky-dory, but the thought of Dezna with one child, enduring the kind of hardships she did, angered me. I felt rage towards those who hurt Dezna, lamented the tears she had to shed, and admired her strength through it all.

Dezna, I realised, perhaps had so much perspective on my parents' own spats, because she, facing greater challenges, had seen the devastation a dysfunctional relationship could wreak on home life.

I tell Winston I want to know about Dezna's relationship with his father. He leans back on the couch, enjoying himself a Guinness Blonde.

"Now, listen, Rossta," he says, pinching the bridge of his nose. "There's a lot you don't know about Mum."

***

Mahogany Hill is a speck of a town, a couple huts lined on a lush hillside with a dirt road that runs through it and leads to higher, still smaller towns.

ANOTHER MOTHER

Dezna, once the little girl who sat for story time with Maas Seamon, has taken to scrubbing the pots, feeding her younger siblings, gathering gungo peas she's picked. She still attends story time until she sips at the grainy dregs of her tea, still hmm-hmm hums verses of "Linstead Market."

But she's growing up, becoming a woman.

It's 1957, and when she walks these hills, the farmers and the miners take notice.

"Haaftanoon, Miss Dezna," they say. "Heevlin', Miss Dezna."

Dezna rises to maturity and autonomy – just as Jamaica itself develops and finds its own growing pains towards independence.

Despite the idyllic simplicity the McDonald household experiences – the stories, the songs, the tea – Jamaica is struggling, slowly dethreading at the seams. The 1930s had brought an economic depression, and demands for political reform arrived when a blight wreaked havoc on the lucrative banana industry such that farmers like Egbert suffered greatly. During Dezna's early childhood, a royal commission scrutinises the state of play in Jamaica from a socioeconomic standpoint and recognises self-government as ideal for the island. Jamaica moves toward independence from the crown. As a result, the island is in flux here by the end of the 1950s. So is Dezna.

Of course, her family is stable, mostly. Egbert is somewhat protected, both geographically and professionally. Though he takes pride in his craftsmanship as a carpenter and in his work as a farmer, the mining of bauxite, the rare red ore abundant in Jamaica and scarce in the rest of the world, provides the security. To extract aluminium from bauxite, foreign firms invest in their Jamaican operations. Alcan, Reynolds, Kaiser Bauxite, Alpart, Revere, and Alcoa all capitalise on Jamaica's reserves of the high-grade ore such that the years 1950–57 see Jamaica grow into the largest bauxite producer in the world. In addition to preaching and carpentry, Egbert works for Revere in St Elizabeth, near the Appleton Estate.

Like her country, Dezna aims for a sense of independence herself and starts to work as a seamstress for the village, setting up shop in her parents' house, bringing a sewing machine out to the veranda. She wets the tip of the thread with her mouth before poking it through the eye of the needle. She is seventeen.

Gervan Buchanan, a local farmer in the community almost twenty-six years her senior, notices the fine work she does out on that porch and makes a point to chat with her. He strokes his scruff when walking by to catch up with the fair-skinned young lady. She knows to keep her distance, just enough: the forty-three-year-old man has quite a reputation as a womaniser in the village, but Dezna has caught his eye and relishes the attention.

The days in Mahogany Hill move slowly. Time extends – torpor setting in among the heat. But in the cool shadow of a porch or under the shade of a moringa tree, time gets slippery and speeds up.

Their relationship happens, like a mini pineapple in the yard: you don't notice it by the veranda, even as it germinates, until suddenly, it's there – spiny, waxen, and cute with just a drop of dew on its crown.

ANOTHER MOTHER

Gervan and Dezna begin an unexpected and torrid romance, as she seeks independence out from under the watchful eye of her parents.

But these years of plenty prove disastrous for the country and strain Gervan's relationship with Dezna. Alcan, Alcoa, and the rest fail to reinvest in other economic sectors, even cramping Jamaica's manufacturing potential by importing their own mining equipment. What's more, though the bauxite industry employs Egbert and some ten thousand others in exploration and open-pit mining, it also hurts employment opportunities for thousands of agricultural workers in rural areas. Dezna watches as bauxite multinational companies buy up land and push small farmers like Gervan out. The companies knock down their houses and use conveyor belts to send their valuable red dirt to ships for the aluminium industry. The tension is palpable. There's little way for Gervan to make a life for himself.

The charm he once demonstrated while he sat with her by the sewing machine on the veranda fades. He sneers. He self-medicates with kick-down.

When Dezna is eighteen, they have their first child, Winston, named after Winston Churchill. It's Gervan's choice. He'll be a boisterous child, Gervan thinks. Hardy. Gervan is something of an anglophile and lacks the Jamaican patriotism Dezna feels, imbued as she is with the notion that independence might solve all this mess. Winston – that's a dignified name fit for a statesman, either way, here on this island of such promise and disquiet.

The country is sacred. The country is scared.

But Dezna foresees a quiet life in Mahogany Hill. Maybe the family can venture to a larger place – Black River, even Montego Bay. She can sew her dresses. Gervan can tend to his fields. But that summer grows long in the face, wearies as fall approaches.

One morning, while she's nursing Winston, Gervan comes out to the porch.

"Mi gone," he says.

"Huh?" Dezna says.

"Yuh *def*? Mi gone."

He has booked passage on a ship to England; he leaves that afternoon as tears stream down her eighteen-year-old face. *Nuh leave me*, she says. *Please, nuh leave me.* But Gervan insists he'll go to England, stay there. He walks away, plants one kiss on Winston's forehead and another on Dezna's as she turns away – the portholes on his steamer like an ellipsis towards her uncertain future. In the years ahead, Gervan will convert to Islam in the UK, change his name to Bashir al Muhammad. All told, he'll have five wives and a couple kids with each throughout his life. He'll return to Jamaica every so often. He'll ask after Miss Dezna, the girl who so assiduously focused on her staystitching, or he won't.

When Gervan leaves, Dezna starts to feel the suffocation in the hills. The romance hadn't gone as she'd imagined. This isn't Mizzy and Tunkey on Lovers' Leap. She returns home to the house of Egbert and Beatrice. She takes care of her mother when she falls ill with cancer. She helps prepare meals for her siblings. She sews dresses and pillow shams and anything else to make order out of the tangled web her life has woven. Her own desire for something greater mirrors the striving Jamaica has for progress, independence – beyond British rule.

She wants to "big up" herself, as is said on the island. She can't be kept in this small village her whole life. The reflex of hope exists in Jamaica. Everything abides by the logic of "soon come".

Montego Bay calls Dezna. She leaves her young Winston with her parents and ventures into the city.

9. Fleeing the Nest

On the blacktop in our Hale Drive driveway when I am eight, I pretend I am at the French Open sliding on the red clay, taking stabs at almost-winners, shovelling them out from ankle height as blasted passing shots. It's difficult to beat the garage door.

I should note: the compressed exhaust of opening the tennis ball can has the fricative *chhh* of Dezna's chiding.

The dented grey edges framing the garage door are most problematic, sending the balls flying off at dramatic angles. In a particularly intense point, the edge shoots back the yellow ball to the right side of the driveway, and I lunge forward, dropping my left shoulder to guide a backhand straight at the door with such fury, I think, as to disrupt the automatic opening system.

Instead, the ball goes straight up the line, missing the gutter, and into the lush vegetation along the front of the house – the pointy yuccas, the lone Japanese maple, stopping short of the weeping cherry by the porch.

ANOTHER MOTHER

Upon snatching the ball from its landing point in a blue star juniper, I realise I have disrupted a hornet's nest. Little needle pricks quickly enter my arms and legs, and I run to escape the attack. I swing my ProKennex racquet around and then drop it on the lawn. I rush along the path to the front porch, kicking over a floodlight or two, and ring the doorbell.

Dezna answers and pulls me, this crying boy, into her chest and shuts the door. On the den's grey couch – the one whose cushions I typically arrange for a change- and crumb-filled cave – she sets up a mini-clinic, like the one she used to run for the Jamaica Ministry of Health.

She takes a warm washcloth and puts pressure on the stings to extract the venom. Dabbing a dollop of cream on a cotton swab, she treats each individual prick. This is just part of what she does, unflinchingly. The kitchen is mopped with ammonia. The lint tray is emptied. The fitted sheets are folded in the linen closet. The boy is comforted.

10. Jamrock-A-Bye

On a cool Friday evening, I meet Orville and Dexter at the Linden, New Jersey, train station – a stop I'd passed many times between Princeton and New York City without ever disembarking. They're waiting for me in a black Nissan Sentra, and I hop in the backseat.

"I hope it's not too cliché, the black guy driving the white guy," Orville says, flashing a disarming grin.

Greying and in his mid-fifties, Orville's broad and built like a retired tight end. He drives buses for New Jersey Transit and has a disciplined disposition and a stoicism built up over decades of dealing with unruly passengers and the frustrations of state government bureaucracy. When he smiles, he has precision dimples. Dexter is a taller, buffer version of his brother and works on the janitorial staff at a hospital; he has a predilection for reggae revival music and Facebook messages involving flowers and hearts.

Orville stares at me, trying to resolve the cognitive dissonance he has between my childhood pictures and the person he sees before him. I perform a similar ritual: I see Dezna in his face – the bulbous nose and bold Maroon cheekbones she inherited from Beatrice, the almond-shaped eyes from Egbert. Dexter has Dezna's sceptical smile, the lips pursed ever so slightly and the right corner of the mouth pulled out and down.

At a local Buffalo Wild Wings, where we order some nachos and Heinekens, I want to learn about Dezna's life post-Gervan in the Montego Bay of the 1960s. But they also want to know the inside story of their mom in New Jersey. They too had a veil on certain aspects of her life with this random family in Princeton.

"I always wondered what it was like for Mum in your house," Orville says.

"Tell us a story about Mum," Dexter insists, his delivery as percussive as Dezna's.

Bath time comes to mind, I tell them. After all, it became an elaborate ritual in 1994 after the release of *Cool Runnings*. Here for years I had this curious connection to a Caribbean country that Princeton families travelled to over school vacations. But the presentation of the Jamaican bobsled team on the big screen augmented interest in the island among people I knew, especially fellow second graders.

All of a sudden, friends imitated the Jamaican accent, quoted the movie.

"*Sanka, yuh dead?*" "*Ya mon…*" emerged as a common call-and-response litany for someone knocked down on the soccer pitch during outdoor recess.

"My babysitter is Jamaican" became instant currency for cool – like Umbro shorts or a "Soccer Is Life…The Rest Is Just Details" T-shirt. "Jamakin' me crazy," boys would say.

But any claim to "Jamaican by association" was met by the peanut gallery with vocal doubt. Announce an affinity for the island, and you'd be labelled as Jafakin'.

At any rate, during that era, Dezna would draw me a warm bath and call me in. In my OCD-addled mind, I always thought it gross to wet my hair in the bathwater, so Dezna would run the faucet with cool water – what I called a Caribbean waterfall. She would crouch over the tub on a salmon-coloured towel while passing a soap-sudded washcloth across my pale back, sloughing off my dead skin into mini greenish-grey coils – my body slathered in lather.

She'd sing her songs – in a hush, the rush of water drowning out most of the lyrics, but not the gentle harmony. Dezna loved to chat too, and she splashed me with her voice, incanted in pedal-held beats. She sounded, at times, like a Shakespearean actor. And her patois washed over me as she cleaned my ears, which were not "dirty" but rather "dutty" in our Jam-Down speech. The bubbles eventually dissolved and formed a filmy layer like the skin of milk on the surface of the bath water.

When Dezna scrubbed my chicken-wing shoulder blades, she expended such care, she might as well have been a master sculptor. Her soothing was an art form.

And with that magical voice, she would sing faintly:
I see woman on bended knee
Cutting cane for her family…

Only years later would I recognise these as lyrics from Harry Belafonte's "Island in the Sun".

The '90s-era New York Knicks were a point of pride for a Jewish young man in the Tri-State area with some vested interest in high-profile Jamaicans, and Dezna and I used bath time to discuss the team, our obsession. Kingston's own Patrick Ewing was, bar none, our saviour. The flattop haircut, the profuse sweating – No. 33 in the Garden, seven feet tall, battling it out against the Michael Jordan-led Chicago Bulls in the Eastern Conference Semis or for the Dream Team – he was awe-inducing.

"Jamaican guy – him," Dezna would say.

That spurred the nationalistic pride – each field goal, each finger-roll over the top strengthened our collective patriotism. The playoffs in '94 were particularly crushing for us, when Ewing failed to capitalise on Jordan's absence from the league that season; the Knicks lost in the finals to the Houston Rockets. Some elementary school kids watched *Sports Center*, but for basketball, I had an in-depth breakdown of every single game – focused, in truth, on a certain player's performance – from my nanny, tubside.

Yet it was after the bath, when my fingertips were nice and pruned, that the true magic began. As I stepped out of the bath – my big toe rubbing the side in a cello hum – she'd drape me in another salmon-coloured towel. I'd complain about the cold air entering through the draughty hallway, and lying down on the floor towel, I'd have one request.

"Dezna, pull me," I'd yell. "*Pull* me."

She would fold me into an elaborate little towel package like a sugar dumpling. And in deference to the hot film at the time, we called this a Jamaican bobsled. Facedown like a frog, my knees tucked to my chest, I'd prepare for liftoff.

"Ready, Maas Ras?" she'd say.

Dezna would yank the front two corners of the towel up over the marble door slab on the floor, dogleg left on the hallway carpet, and speed another left into my cosy room. Fifteen seconds of thrill. Sometimes I'd stay in there a minute or two – so cuddled and free from care – before getting dressed.

Some years later, it was a sad day when I became too heavy to be pulled. But even now, being stuck at a bus stop underdressed in unseasonably cold weather or caught in a frigid downpour in some remote part of Scandinavia can trigger a synapse summoning that cotton toboggan.

Orville and Dexter laugh – imagining their mother counting down like we were in an Olympic race and yanking me through the hallway.

"All right," I say. "Your turn."

They hesitate a bit: Orville purses his mouth and squints his eyes, averting them, and Dexter darts his glance side to side between Orville and me as if watching a game of ping-pong.

But soon enough the two brothers, leaning their elbows on the grated table and rounding their shoulders forward, settle in to tell me about Dezna's life in Montego Bay.

***

ANOTHER MOTHER

They call him Cope.

Cornelius Cope is a handsome chef and not a half-bad cricket batsman. Dashing and six-two, he's a hurry-come-up in the hotel industry who cooks and tends bar at high-class tourist locations: Coral Cliff, Upper Deck, Round Hill. He puts Scotch bonnet peppers in every dish, minces them up and fans them out on the edge of a plate with his blade. The tourists feel the burn right in their philtrum, between their nose and upper lip – precision spice. He makes a mean kick-down with high ABV steel bottom but can also mix a Sazerac, into which he sprinkles some bitters, that will knock you out.

He smiles when he slams a rocks glass down on the bar.

"Evening vespers...," he says, delighted as he watches American tourists get increasingly schnockered. This is 1960 in this quirky quasar when Jamaica resorts are booming. The actor Errol Flynn, an island enthusiast, promotes the trend, and many American and British luminaries are travelling to Jamaica, in part for medical tourism. The main hotels double as sanitoriums – a place for the rich to decompress, cure what ails them, drink some stiff rum. *Come to Jamaica and feel all right.*

At Coral Cliff Hotel and Entertainment Resort, Cope's first gig in the industry, the tagline is: "Simply Exciting. Simply Entertaining. Simply Exhilarating." Overlooking the Hip Strip and near Doctor's Cave Beach, it's a scene, even if the St James Parish Council, at the expense of the Montego Bay Hotels Association, often fogs the hotel area with Dieldrex to eliminate mosquitoes. That takes nothing away from the classiness of the ambience and the sense of cool, that is, in the parlance of the time, *bad like yaws*. When Cope works here a couple days a week, he observes Coral Cliff is strewn with neckties and silver salvers of cocktails. The proprietress, Mrs J.H. Clarke, guarantees "viands of the freshest and daintiest". During the day, contrails scrape the sky over the beach. Come evening, when guests twist a bottle of wine into the sand and sit on the lilos and chaises longues to hear the waves crash, they can see the phosphorescence aglow in the Caribbean Sea. High above hangs a scallop moon.

Dezna has fled the hills and come to the North Coast, with just one straw bag of her belongings – mostly the dresses she's made – and her sewing machine. She can't take Winston to the Second City and make a life for herself, so after a year of nursing, she leaves him with Egbert and Beatrice, gives him a kiss on the forehead. She misses the afternoon-picked papaya, the ripe Julie mango, the agapanthus flowers, the flitting peeny-wallies. But she's taken a room of her own and set up shop as a dressmaker. She puts a little wooden placard in the window on which she's painted "Miss Dezna – Seamstress" in violet. She has bead curtains in her doorway and toils away on pant cuffs and wedding dresses, hoping one day to make her own.

Country girl has come to the big city, and she teems with excitement for what she can accomplish. Dezna is nineteen and ready to elevate her station in life. She's prepared for jump-off-a-cliff-for-you love. If those nights on Egbert's veranda did anything for her, they made her a supreme dreamer.

ANOTHER MOTHER

She walks through MoBay in her daily wanderings as the trade wind blows through the city, sees White Witch Rose Hall atop the hill, putters around Sam Sharpe Square in her ballet flats. She likes to feel the ground on her feet; it reminds her of her years of walking the hills in St Elizabeth among the guava and tamarind trees, the lignum vitae blooming. She feels the kindness of strangers but also the strangeness of kindness.

Cope is nineteen years Dezna's senior, exactly twice her age – and she becomes his *boonoonoonoos*. When they meet for the first time – at the behest of Philip, Cope's brother who lives catty-corner from Egbert in Mahogany Hill – Dezna feels more at ease than she otherwise might have. The family connection allows her to breathe evenly when she stops by his apartment at 39 Market Street. Cope cuts an impressive figure when he comes to the door – a monumental man, whose imposing presence makes him appear three or four inches taller than he really is. She has come, and he is gladdened. He's a chain smoker, lighting his next Craven "A" cigarette with the stub of his last as they chat until he's depleted the entire red-and-white box. When he offers her a Red Stripe, she scroonches her lips to her nose with disgust and embellishes the gesture with a head shake.

"Not much of a drinker?" Cope says, with a heh of a chuckle.

"Not of beer," she says. "White rum only."

There is an immediate attraction and yet a necessity to go through the motions – asking after each other's family, reminiscing about their roots. The conversational dance. The encircling each other with talk of country, of village characters from *dung di rohd*. The afternoon is getting warmer as it does periodically when the day moves toward dusk, and through the window, frigate birds in the sky appear the shape of flung scissors. Cope has to get to work on a shuttle to tend bar for the dinner shift at another resort. Dezna walks out with him, daydreams around Overton Plaza. She carries a small canvas dulcimina suitcase to put her produce in and walks with it slung around her shoulder as she saunters through lanes and catches the breeze lazily wafting in from the sea.

At Round Hill in Hanover's Hopewell, Cope shines, comes into his element. Grace Kelly is a frequent guest, and Noël Coward and Clive Brock stay in "world-weary bungalows". There are two black-tie nights each week, and easy Monday night beach parties gather film stars, polo players, and titans of industry around a sizzling barbecue while a Calypso band plays on the patio.

Totlyn Jackson, Jamaica's "First Lady of Song", is often draped over the piano while Baba Motta and the boys, the Zodiacs, play to create a seductive nightclub atmosphere. With her sultry soprano, the one she honed at the North Street Cathedral in Kingston, Jackson croons "Island in the Sun" and "Yellow Bird" as Cope shakes drinks – Hummingbirds and, of course, Sazeracs.

The Duke of Marlborough is a regular. As is Fred Astaire's sister, Adele. The producer George Minter stops by from time to time, and Cope knows to make his drinks extra stiff but not to serve him too many.

Viscount Esmond Rothermere, heir to the *Daily Mail* newspaper enterprise, buys Cottage 16 so that his wife, Lady

ANOTHER MOTHER

Anne Rothermere, and he can enjoy some steamy getaways, but James Bond author Ian Fleming is said to have been the one pleasing the lady in the cottage behind the viscount's back. JFK and Jackie Kennedy famously honeymoon in Round Hill's four-bedroom Villa 10 and return several times to enjoy the private pool, expansive lawn, and sweeping views of the nature beyond the resort. Cope claims to have mixed him a strawberry daiquiri.

Here, the atmosphere is soaked in navy-proof grandeur and British charm. The one hundred-acre peninsula of the resort once was part of a sugarcane plantation known as Lord Monson's Round Hill Estate. And lush is the bluff's soil, which provides an ideal growing area for coconuts, Jamaican allspice, and pineapples. Given that Round Hill's logo is the pineapple, Dezna is drawn to Cope, seeing the connection as a sign. Pineapple, that colonial symbol of hospitality, welcoming in a new future.

The fanciness of Round Hill is a rarefied world away from humble Mahogany Hill. Montego Bay is swinging. It erupts in flamboyant yellows and reds and purples and greens, golden rays of ska sax flexing through the greyscale of alleyways and then evaporating. Everything in Jamaica is shining. Take Phosferine, ads read, "for extra strength, vitality, and strong nerves." And in Jamaica, too, just about every herb is a form of Viagra. Moringa, a flowering tree native to the sub-Himalayas, is a potent aphrodisiac and all over the island. Combine Moringa with quail eggs? That's an extra stiff proposition.

Medina, another herb, is not for the faint of heart. Jamaica is flourishing, and with each cross-stitch Dezna makes and each tumbler Cope fills, they're coming closer to the life they want – a more comfortable one with fewer worries. But the island's own hakuna matata, *Don't worry 'bout a thing* — that's a disguised Jamaican attitude. You *have* to worry. Optimism can be foolish, callow. Expect the unexpected. Cover your batty.

Dezna embraces life with Cope, even as Jamaica moves toward independence and uncertainty swirls throughout the island. They live there at 39 Market Street in a humble apartment across from Sam Isaac & Son Funeral Home. He smokes his Craven "A"s by the window, and she puts her clapboard sign out facing the street. They are handling the challenges together. His last name, Dezna notes, is even a verb that describes how she's endured and managed hardship.

Dezna is heavily pregnant when Cope and she join the gathering crowd to celebrate Jamaica's independence on August 6, 1962. Come September 18, she gives birth to Orville while Cope is shaking drinks at Round Hill. Her son may have a fancy British name, but he'll be a Jamaican through and through, she says. The island is now a former British colony, after all.

Extreme change is afoot throughout the island as it emerges from British rule and seeks to create its own destiny. There is great economic hope and nationwide optimism, particularly under Prime Minister Alexander Bustamante, but also uncertainty. That trickles down to Dezna's household, and her relationship with Cope is on the fritz even as she gets pregnant in 1963 with her third child.

ANOTHER MOTHER

Dezna wants to get married. Her feet are glued to the earth, but her head is in the clouds with stories, with idealisations. Her man is handsome, hardworking. He has a hearty laugh, cooks a mean meal, mixes a strong rum cocktail.

"Why we nuh get married?" she asks him, nearly every day.

He's just about reached forty years old without needing to put a ring on his finger. Why not leave well enough alone? Cope barrels through life the way he barrels through doorways – haphazardly, knowing he can withstand the obstacles that come in his way without foresight, without being locked down to a set plan. He has served millionaires, Hollywood royalty, an American president. He's content to smoke his Craven "A"s between sips of Red Stripe.

When Dezna has Dexter in May of 1964, she is nursing her baby, caring for two-year-old Orville, making elaborate dresses for the women of Montego Bay, and looking after Cope. He works later and later at Round Hill. He takes on additional shifts to earn that extra money. To hustle in Jamaica is a national sport. He's a large, handsome man. He's quiet but charismatic. Quick with a grin at the bar. Dezna keeps her faith, hoping Cope will turn around, commit himself to this little family they've built themselves, the one she envisioned when she first arrived in Montego Bay. She orders her life through stitches, measures it through feedings. She consumes almost nothing, just cups of tea with a sprinkle of salt. This isn't the bush she's used to in country, just Tetley black brew. Dexter looks like a carbon copy of his father. He's a man-child, large. She's grateful for her children, for the children Cope has given her. The days are routine, the afternoons announced by the carnival music of the peanut vendor's cart.

But Dezna and Cope are squabbling. Money is tighter, and it's getting harder for an individual to make a substantial income without the economic stewardship of the British government. Enterprises lack funding and oversight, and the hotel industry, in particular, tightens its belt on its employees. Cope works hard, exhausts himself for less and less. And he comes home to meals that are increasingly simple. He gets up and does it again, for rewards that are all the more meagre.

But Cope can chat. Cope can chat, all right. But those extra tips at the bar aren't going to compensate for the loss. He too comes from the hills. He's of St Elizabeth stock, and he's made a life for himself in MoBay. He cannot be contained. He bursts out of uniforms. Church blazers he tears – his shoulders are just too broad. He rips slacks with his too-long strides. Dezna tries to mend breaches, darn them. But Dezna with her pieties and grievances cannot contain Cope.

"Mi cyant anymahr," Dezna says, finally. "Mi cyant."

For Dezna, love and despair are too often concomitant forces.

With tensions in the city intensifying, her relationship with Cope is officially over. She takes her two children and flees back to the hills.

11. Mother of Invention

Dear Dezna,

This search has been a strenuous one.

I have immersed myself in your life, in your past, about which I knew so little.

In a series of happy accidents and who-whudda-thunk-its, you appeared at our doorstep during a blizzard. You were a stranger at first. You became another mother.

I am writing, like you always wanted. I do not need to be told to do so.

I have been to Mahogany Hill and run my fingers along your home's sideboards, trying to absorb some of your energy, attempting to understand you. I have met your children and searched for your face in their features, the survival of your essence in mouth-to-the-side smiles and furrowed brows.

I have explored your path through the 1940s, and '50s, and '60s, and '70s, and '80s. And I have spelunked through the corners of my own memory to access our cherished time together and record it.

Every day, I think about you, about your lessons imprinted upon me. The striving, the work ethic, the humility. O.K. – I'm working on the humility.

I am relying on my hyperthymesia, trying to access our shared past each day even as I wander with uneven footing along the terrain of your hidden life. I find myself returning to specific episodes throughout my childhood with you and tripping on the roots of memory along the way. Little by little, I am strip-mining the past, making sense of its abstractions as if gazing through the kaleidoscopic View-Master we used to use.

I am five. I am a spy. I am walking around the house with a leather briefcase that is actually just a fancy, fold-up-able backgammon board. My grandfather and uncle have died in the last year, and as I approach the kitchen where you are watching *The Young and the Restless*, I drop the game set.

"Dezna, I'm sad about dying," I say.

"Oh, Ras-mon," you say. "Come here…"

"I don't want to die," I say as you embrace me.

"You have a hundred years of life ahead of you. Make the most of your time in this world."

I am eight. I can see you're shy, scrunching your face – your mouth and eyes pressed in like a tufted cushion toward the button of your nose – when I ask who's on the phone.

You are on the cordless at the bottom of the basement stairs and sound giddy, there among the workout mats and dumbbells, a NordicTrack, and a stationary bike with a twist-screw lock. We are supposed to be watching WWF, with its clotheslines and haymakers, and folding the laundry together. We favour the Undertaker (whose tagline "Expect the Unexpected" we playfully use with each other in a deep register) and Randy Savage (though we categorically hate Slim Jim commercials).

You just hand me the receiver.

"Say hello…"

"Hello," I say.

"Wah gwaan?" says the Barry White voice on the other end of the line.

The man's speech pops quickly in iambic Jamtameter, a kindly bass with subwoofer amplification that hits my ears with that oontz-oontz-oontz. I throw you a surprised glance, and you dart your eyes downward as you smile. I feel like I've stolen the Saab for a joy-ride down the driveway, experiencing the rush of something from the forbidden adult world.

My voice is eunuch-on-helium squeaky, so the man thinks I'm my sister. I'm embarrassed and correct him. You laugh. I am so nervous to be speaking to a stranger.

After a few more pleasantries, I pass the phone back to you.

I ask again who this is, and you change your tone a little – your giggles morph to a strained smile.

"A no ebry kin teet a laaf," you say, as always. *Showing the skin of your teeth doesn't always mean a laugh.* I now understand that you can't interpret every smile as a sign of genuine amusement.

Here in the basement, your life is kept below the surface.

My role as a little brother has made me nosy, but I get it. I launch up the stairs to watch more wrestling.

I wear the One Love threaded bracelet you brought back from your island, and I use the souvenir reggae pencil with a knit cap and dreadlocks hanging from the eraser to do my homework. I store it in my Deluxe Drawer, with my grandfather's watch, a Kiddush cup, a buffalo nickel, a basketball participation medal, and a piggy bank filled with Jamaican coins and a Jamaican one-dollar bill with Alexander Bustamante on the face (I keep it in my wallet to this day).

I am nine. My mother says I will be a surgeon. That's because we sew all the time – yellow felt pillows stuffed with the cotton we usually pulled apart to spread on bushes for Halloween spider webs. You taught me to lick the end of the thread and grind it ever so slightly between my teeth to give it a point to pass through the eye of the needle before cinching a slipknot. You execute with a fancy cross-stitch as you hum and *The Sally Jessy Raphael Show* blares in the background. When *Ricki Lake* comes on, I learn what a one-night stand is. I'm getting an education. It's no big deal; I am just sewing in uneven pick-stitch. And even though I understand, I test the waters and ask you anyway about the term. You laugh and provide a simple, non-explicit explanation. Thank you for treating me like an adult but respecting my innocence. I continue sewing.

All the while, we are counting in the Jamaican way you taught me, in a little song:

> *One and twenty, two and twenty, three and four and five and six and twenty. Twenty-seven. Twenty-eight. Twenty-nine. Thirty. One and thirty, two and thirty, three and four and five and six and thirty. Thirty-seven. Thirty-eight. Thirty-nine. Forty....*

ANOTHER MOTHER

That day, I am also working on a Boy Scouts project, in which we are tasked with creating an object to serve as a mnemonic device. You help me sew a mini messenger bag with a bell on it. It is royal blue with a triangular piece of red felt to suggest an envelope fold and circular yellow felt mock buttons, whose fringes betray the black Sharpie marks I had made to outline my scissor cutting. They appear green on the yellow felt. Every time you hear the bag ring, you are supposed to remember something you forgot. You keep me on task in creating it. "You come yah fi drink milk, you no come yah fi count cow!" you say, as always. Focus on the goal, the important matters – not the extraneous. The bag outshines my blue and gold Pine Box Derby car from the previous year.

All the while, you take breaks to carry the laundry basket on your head when ascending the stairs to put the clothes away in the bedrooms. You say the secret lies in a sturdy neck and the maintenance of squared shoulders. But when I try that day, my toothpick neck snaps with a plink, and warm, freshly folded laundry crashes on the already scratched landing.

I bring my pillow and mnemonic device bag with me into my room that night. I always insist on using my pillow creations under my head in bed even though you mention that might not be a great idea as you tuck me in with my teddy bear, Hammer – a nod to my father's hardware store. There is a tear on his left foot where I hide the key to my piggy bank. The moon is lambent through my window as I chew through a yawn. You tickle my back and sing.

Red and yellow, black and white,
Jesus loves the Israelite...

I wake up with a sore neck, of course, and you undo my stitching to add another bag of cotton fluff to my pillow.

I deke left in my mind. I am twenty-one. On the phone in my Princeton dorm room my senior year, a few months after our last Thanksgiving together, I call you to tell you I've been offered an internship at *The Wall Street Journal*.

"I always knew, Ras-mon," you say. "I always knew."

I have a thesis to write, and the kids you watch are returning from school soon. We don't have much time.

The Knicks are terrible, I mention.

"No playoffs this year," you say.

"It's not so much the Patrick Ewing days anymore."

How I yearned for the time when a Jamaican seven-footer ruled New York and a formidable Jamaican woman captained our own Urken squad of five.

These days, everyone is working hard, Dezna. We want to do you proud. Maxine is harvesting papayas and selling them well in downtown Montego Bay near the bakery Time and Patience, an appropriate name given the line down the block its customers always form as baguettes lie napping in the window. But don't get me started on the sweet Easter bun they sell there – why did you hide that treasure from me all my life? I am meeting everyone from Mahogany Hill – Dragon, Junior, the village hermit who is harmless and, it seems, kind of sweet.

ANOTHER MOTHER

A refreshing jelly on a hot day in the heart of St. Elizabeth confirms for me the existence of some higher power. I wish I could call you and give you an update on all of this. As time goes onward, we're all making something of ourselves. I wish we could, if briefly, commiserate about the Knicks.

I'm trying to tie this series of concatenated events together in my mind to link past and present. I think to our time sitting on the front porch and watching cecropia moths flitter about the lamps and fireflies turn on and off intermittently across the front yard. You say the stars twinkle because of wind gusts. I feel such equipoise. The morning moments of butter melting in Cream of Wheat. The nightly tickled tuck-ins when your words might as well have been the Beatitudes. You are a constant, a sloop in the harbour. The past speeds forth in fast-forwarded chipmunk voices as I cull through it at various time stamps. It's a dizzying process, mental theme-park teacups. Recollections of our time together hit me like blow darts – multiple times a day. I keep pinch-potting the past in my mind, scoring the edges to make connections. I am wading out in the littoral region of my memory, grasping at engrams. My words are not enough, but they are what you've given me. They are my true riches, growing over time – that I might turn the surplus over to you.

I have more journeying left in this quest. But let me just say: I miss you, and I love you.

Always,

Ras-mon

12. Blue-Blue

The Friday night before Dezna's grandson Dymar (aka Blue-Blue) is set to arrive at our one-bedroom apartment on the Upper West Side, I am frantically Windexing the mirrors in our bathroom with squeaky swipes and Swiffering the kitchen floor. The sheets that have been sitting in a drawer, I've laundered so they'd be fresh. Just eleven years old, Dymar had taken his first-ever flight, and by himself, from Montego Bay to Newark earlier in the week to stay with Orville and his family during part of his summer vacation.

But Maxine wants him to spend some time in New York City with "Uncle Ross and Aunt Tiff", so we've arranged to have him bunk with us to explore the Big Apple. We've done some extra grocery shopping, and I've cleaned and filled the percolator with water and Blue Mountain coffee so it's ready to plug in when Orville drops off Dymar.

After I brush my teeth, I notice there is a bit of emerald build-up at the base of the faucet, the result of water on metal. So I take a floss stick and use the sharp end to trace a circle and chip away at the crud, unnoticeable to normal-person eyes. I then wipe away the debris with a Kaboom-soaked paper towel. I'm about to head to bed where Tiffan is reading but decide to go the extra mile and use a toilet brush in the bowl with some Clorox. I vigorously scrub around the bowl and, in my haste as I'm cleaning, dislodge the brush part from the handle. The toilet suctions it down. I try to reach my hand in, but the bristly bit is too far away. I spring over to my closet and grab a metal coat hanger, which I untwist and MacGyver into an extended hook. In my enthusiasm, I manage to push the brush even deeper into the hole and over a drop-off, at which point it's no longer possible to pull it back. *Maybe if I just flush it down*, I think, as any genius would. So I pull the metal lever. At these sorts of moments, we become extra religious, and I hold my breath. The toilet flushes normally but then slows. A small pool of bleachy water has collected at the bottom of the bowl and doesn't fully drain for a good ten seconds. Then, with some gurgling, it lowers into the depths, so the bowl is waterless. By some miracle, the tank resolves the water to its normal standing level. I let forth a sigh of relief, then shrug my shoulders and beam with satisfaction at myself in the mirror. I wash my hands four times.

"What's wrong?" Tiffan says as I crawl into bed.

"Nothing – just making sure everything is ready."

She shuts off her night-table lamp.

A knock on our door wakes me at seven in the morning.

As I stumble out to the front hall, I see an inch of water –

clean water, mercifully – standing in the bathroom from the overflowing toilet.

I look through the peep hole to see my burly super and open the door.

"You make flood in gym," he says in his Albanian accent.

I mumble an apology. He grumbles and rubs his ham-hock-sized hand through his buzz cut. Then he enters my bathroom with a snake and a type of wrench whose name I forget that I used to sell at my dad's hardware store. Dymar will be here in two hours.

I grab some paper towels and soon thereafter switch to bath towels to sop up the water. My super stabilises the flood. And it is with horror that I watch him chisel around the caulking and upend the toilet from its base, then move it across the bathroom.

He removes the bristly culprit from what is a hole in the ground and inspects it in his hand. He shakes his head, then raises his eyebrows at me.

I go red in the face.

Then he resecures the toilet to its original position in the tile.

I frantically wring the soaked bathmat out into the tub, throw the towels I've used into the laundry basket, pour bleach on the tile, and Swiffer again.

By the time Orville and Dymar arrive, I open the door out of breath and cartoonishly lean my elbow against the wall and grin, darting my eyes to the extremities of my peripheral vision as if to play innocent.

I greet them both with a hug and put the coffee on.

Dymar, who is wearing navy blue cargo shorts and a T-shirt the same colour, is about four-eight. On the right lens of his thick-framed spectacles, there is a fishbone-sized scratch. He has broad shoulders and tends to bend forward at the waist like Maxine so as to acquire an aspect of inspecting, an at-the-ready ability to observe. He often scroonches up his nose like Dezna and stares straight ahead like she did when in deep thought.

"So riddle me this," I say. "What do I call you, Dymar or Blue-Blue?"

"Whichever works," he says.

In Jamaica, everyone has a nickname called a Yard name. You might know someone for years named Donny and assume that his given name is Donald or maybe, at the very least, his middle name is. But then you see his ID, and no, his name is Jeffrey Nesta.

Nicknames in Jamaica just happen. When I ask Orville about the origin of this nickname, he shrugs his shoulders. "He just always wear blue."

"Did Dezna have a nickname?"

"Zezna," Orville responds.

"Zezna," I say.

Blue-Blue enters deeper into the apartment and slings his overnight backpack on the couch, settles in, and asks for the WiFi password.

"I can't cook dumpling, but I can make a mean omelette," I say.

Tiffan comes out as I'm in front of the stove, and Blue-Blue gives her a big hug.

As we eat, he is obsessively interested in our likes and dislikes.

"*Whish* you pree-fer – *mahr* di dog or *mahr* di cat?" Blue-Blue says.

The questions keep coming.

"*Mahr* di Ferrari or *mahr* di Lamborghini?"

"*Mahr* di KFC or *mahr* di McDonald's?"

Orville heads back to Jersey, and Tiffan, Blue-Blue, and I walk up to the American Museum of Natural History. Blue-Blue, like many Jamaican men, carries a washcloth to dab at the beads of sweat that appear on his forehead in the summer heat. Once inside, we pretend we're archaeologists as we move past the dinosaur bones.

We stroll through Central Park to go to the Metropolitan Museum of Art and walk through the Egyptian section and see the sculpture installation on the roof. We go kayaking on the Hudson, then get the burgers and concretes he's been wanting to try at Shake Shack.

This leads to another "*Whish you pree-fer...?*"

We go to a street fair with churros and fresh-squeezed lemonade, and soon, a loud bass lures us to a dark tent, inside of which T-shirts pulsate with neon electricity in alignment with the music. He's mesmerised and picks out a shirt with a design depicting an old-school boom box whose volume-level measurements light up. We walk along the Hudson by the

Intrepid back home. Along the way, he holds up his cell phone to his T-shirt and blasts music just to make sure it still works.

Tiffan wants to have Bolognese and salad for dinner followed by sundaes, and when she gets that started, Blue-Blue makes a request.

"Do you have any Funyuns?"

"Funyuns?" I say.

"You know, the chips…" he says.

"We don't…but we can try to go find some," Tiffan says, looking at me with amusement.

While I tend to the stove, Tiffan and Dymar journey the Upper West Side to track down his favourite snack. They try a Western Beef grocery store, a gourmet market called Gracefully. They go to one bodega, then another. No dice. They land in the back aisle of a third bodega and still can't find any. They head to a Duane Reade – still nothing. Then they finally give up and get Oreos and Doritos at CVS.

Blue-Blue is not *not* upset.

"Well, you can't say we didn't try," Tiffan says.

He does take comfort in the snacks once Tiffan and he arrive back at the apartment, and we extend our drop-leaf table to have a nice meal together. But Blue-Blue has eaten a few too many chips and eats only a small portion of his dinner. He starts yawning as we enjoy some small sundaes, and I pull out the couch to make up his bed.

Tiffan and I have become the babysitters.

Blue-Blue moves towards the pull-out bed to plop down, but I call out abruptly.

Blue-Blue

"Brush and flush, Blue-Blue," I say.

Once he's finished in the bathroom, Tiffan and I stand on either side of the bed and pull the comforter up to his shoulders.

"Should we sing you a lullaby?" I say.

"I'm too old for that," he says.

The next day when I take the train with Blue-Blue to Linden to bring him back to Orville, we sit on the drab New Jersey Transit seats on the Northeast Corridor line.

I hand Blue-Blue his ticket so he can give it to the conductor himself.

When the conductor comes by our row, she looks confusedly at the eleven-year-old boy she thinks, for a moment, is travelling all by himself.

"We're…" I say, oscillating my pointer finger back and forth between Blue-Blue and me.

"Oh, you're…" she says, swivelling her pointer and middle fingers between us in a horizontal bunny ears shape.

"Yes," I say and smile.

13. Waah Good

*I*n March 2016, Tiffan and I are in West Palm Beach where she is in a musical, so we contact May, Dezna's second-oldest daughter, who works as a caretaker at a ritzy kosher assisted-living facility there. Orville and Dexter could only take me so far in understanding Dezna's life during her MoBay years; I want to meet May as another touch point to connect with my nanny but also as a means to understand her life once she retreated back to the hills of St Elizabeth.

I invite May's family out to dinner, but she insists on having us over.

"It's Sunday," she texts. "We island people love to cook. Smile."

Her husband, Desmond, puts on Bob Marley's *Legend* when Tiffan and I arrive at their apartment, and Diamond, their six-year-old daughter, grabs us by the hands to pull us into the living room. She never really lets go.

May and I hug, and I match her features, her smile to those of her sisters and, in aggregate, back to Dezna's face. May has

Marcelled hair that she's given volume through tightly wound curlers, and she wears a Kelly green blouse.

"This is a long time coming," Desmond says.

Desmond, who has a grizzled goatee and an uneven gait, met May by complete accident. A couple months after her first marriage ended, she dialled the wrong number when trying to call a friend while back in Jamaica from Florida.

"I'm so sorry," she said over the receiver. "I have the wrong number."

"No, you don't," he boomed in his baritone.

"I meant to…"

"There are no coincidences."

They talked for another two hours. Then had more calls. Then finally met for a date

May and Desmond have a mezuzah in their West Palm Beach apartment – not on the doorframe, just there on the counter. And a Kiddush cup. And a menorah. These are all gifts residents of the old-folks home gave to May.

"They're all a little meshuganah," she says.

Ever since this visit, she's texted me to celebrate holidays I don't really know about: "Happy Tisha B'Av!" she writes. "O.K.!" I think, as I smile widely.

I'd be going to Jamaica in another month or so for the laying of Dezna's headstone, and May wants to know if I ever travelled to Jamaica as a child.

Almost, I tell her. One morning, my mother wakes me up with a glass of orange juice with a curious blue pill dissolving into the liquid like a Dalí sunrise. I am fourteen, and my mother is trying to roofie me. (My mother has never uttered an apologetic phrase. If I ever hear her say "I'm sorry," I'll brief you. It is then we'll know the end of times is nigh.)

My mom wants me to get on a plane to Jamaica, where she's planned a vacation with my sister and me at the Ritz-Carlton Montego Bay while my dad minds the store. Of course, I had advised her in advance that I wouldn't be flying.

"Ross has a fear of flying," she'd tell people.

"I have a fear of death."

I can't explain why exactly, but I have always suffered from aviophobia. There's an element of discomfort in losing control. I also had been haunted by my Uncle Todd's untimely death in a helicopter.

That morning, my mother forces me to get dressed and in the car with Kurt, the Chevron-moustached policeman my father knows who drives us to the airport on our vacations.

My mother has a Chanel scarf tied around her neck. Her most dramatic statements are always sartorial (and bought at *bahhgain* prices). She instructs Kurt on how to position the one suitcase specifically dedicated to her shoes. She uses the same tone as in restaurants when sending soup back to be warmed "piping hot" without first testing the temperature.

When we get to the Philadelphia airport, I refuse to get out of the car.

"*Rooaws*, it's only a four-hour flight," she says.

"It doesn't matter," I say.

My mother finally gives up when the time to get to the gate grows short. I cry, from the medication, the lack of sleep, the turmoil of being coerced into a situation that puts me ill at ease.

After my mother and sister leave, Kurt looks at me as I blubber. He turns on the radio and lands upon the classical music station.

"How's this?" he says.

"Fine," I sniffle.

We sit there for some thirty seconds in silence before he hits the dash.

"I can't listen to this shit," he says, changing the station. I giggle a little.

He puts the car in drive and presses the pedal down, heading towards Princeton.

That trip my sister and mother meet Maxine and treat her to a coffee and snack at the Ritz's White Witch restaurant, and I spend the week with my father as snow blankets New Jersey.

May laughs at the story, my childhood neuroses.

"Well, you're making up for lost time," she says.

I am indeed immersing myself in Jamaica as an adult and at this moment cannot fully anticipate how my world will soon be rocked during our trip to Dezna's grave.

But I have only so much power to wade into Dezna's history by myself. I'm trying to conjure up the past I never experienced. In my conversations with Dezna's family members and the people of the hills, I begin to internalise the struggles Dezna went through and imagine her emotional fitness ever strengthening despite the economic challenges walloping her country and family.

This sondage also allows me to see patterns in how she raised me. Dezna and I would explore the forests surrounding our neighbourhood or invent games with tennis balls and the spiky seeds from a sweetgum tree; my ability to learn of Dezna's history brings into relief her own creativity in keeping me engaged and entertained. To get true insight into Dezna's journey, I have to gain clarity on another era of her life as I try to Sticky Tack everything together.

"I'm missing a link to the time spent at Bready's house, the Pisgah days," I say.

So over a meal of jerk chicken and roasted breadfruit as Diamond, Desmond, Tiffan, and I listen, May tells me about a life where, from the veranda, there are pineapple groves as far as the eye can see.

***

After Dezna leaves Cope in Montego Bay and returns to Mahogany Hill with Orville and Dexter, she arrives and buries her head in Maas Seamon's chest. He's aged plenty in the three years since she went away, and his white face is tan and leathery from the summer. He sits down on his cedar rocking chair and gestures toward the empty chair for Dezna to join him, as young Rohena watches from the yard.

Denza feels as if she's failed – two relationships down the drain. Her big city dreams have gone bust. Country girl comes to town and turns right around back to country. Those evenings lying in bed with Cope – as he has just one more Craven "A" until it burns down towards his lips as he sleeps and she plucks it out – feel so far away. The jangle of the beaded curtain when she first got to the city, her "Seamstress" clapboard sign painted in violet. The one night at Round Hill when she put on the fanciest polka dot dress she made and Cope served her a rye-filled Sazerac among the glitterati as white caps crashed far from shore. She knew what it was like to feel like a queen, even fleetingly. The way the crowd moved down to the sugary-sand beach, dotted with cowries and whelk shells, to see the phosphorescence in the water – she'd always remember.

That was then. She's returned here to St Elizabeth by train. Somehow, she's managed the whole way without crying. But the brackish tears flow when she steps foot on McDonald Farm here in Mahogany Hill.

"Ebry mikkle mek a mukkle," Maas Scamon says. Every little bit counts towards progress. She can't focus on the past. And he offers a new spin on a Jamaican sensibility: Why worry when you can pray?

Plus, Dezna doesn't really have the opportunity to perseverate on bygones. She has three young boys to raise and her mother's cancer to treat.

In 1960s Jamaica, you don't really go to the doctor. That would be crazy. What you do instead is simple: ignore it. Or drink some cerasee tea. If something is systemically wrong with you, maybe it will pass. Just maybe you can science it away with obeah.

ANOTHER MOTHER

Dezna, though given to fantasy, is too much of a realist to buy into alternative medicine that much. Beatrice needs actual modern medicine to help cure her, and Dezna invites a doctor she knows from Montego Bay to visit Beatrice. He instructs Dezna on how and when to administer certain tablets and treatments, how to guide Beatrice's diet, how to monitor her condition.

Dezna is taking care of her three children, her three younger siblings, her sick mother. She's tired. She blinks, and she's turned twenty-four. She's cooking meals, washing baby clothes, helping Rohena with her reading assignments, giving pills to her mother, picking gungo peas, scrubbing pots. This is what it means to be a *sufferah*. She prays her life will get easier. She wants to find a way to improve herself, one she'd hoped the big city would provide.

During the doctor's next visit, he notices Beatrice's improved condition and Dezna's painstaking care for her mother. He observes how intuitive Dezna is with her mother's health care, how she anticipates certain complications and how she might keep them at bay.

"You should be a doctor," he tells her.

"Well, I thought of becoming a nurse," she says.

And so she's cooking meals, washing baby clothes, helping Rohena with her reading assignments, giving pills to her mother, and studying for her nurse's examination from the Ministry of Health. She's reading the books on the veranda during the day, and she's looking at them by the light of a kerosene lamp as Maas Seamon leads his story time.

Soon enough she passes the tests, and she's a sister nurse working the hills, going door to door.

One day when making a house call to a squat bachelor thirteen years her senior – a *fawma*, specialising in pineapples – she provides him with some tablets to lower his blood pressure.

"O.K., Mistah Sanderson," she says, giving his knee two staccato taps before her customary goodbye: "Likkle more…"

He smells like musk and has a trim, grizzled beard, she's noticed. It is stuffy in his dwelling, too hot. Life here is different from in Montego Bay where she used to walk in her ballet flats through Sam Sharpe Square. The trade wind that blows through Montego Bay off the water had invigorated her. Back in the hills, she's starting to feel suffocated. She doesn't want to be pinned down. And yet.

George knows a bit about Miss Dezna's story. He's heard about how that louse Gervan ran off to England. He hears that guy changed his name, got another wife, maybe a third or fourth by this time. He knows Miss Dezna went to Montego Bay with so much promise. He's seen her work. He's attended story gatherings at Maas Seamon's house.

Dezna knows of Bready. It's a small enough village, but she's never really interacted with him. Nursely work, though, is intimate. Providing care is personal. The nurturing is something to which people naturally respond. It's a connection between someone who provides a service and someone who has a need.

She pats his thigh one more time. In the heat of the moment, his heart beats faster, and there in his little hut, they exchange a slow kiss.

ANOTHER MOTHER

"Wa'ppun?" she says, startled by what has occurred.

She pauses, then removes her Coke-bottle glasses and leans back in to embrace him. She is so tired. Walking the hills, caring for her mother, caring for her patients, caring for her babies. She's overwhelmed, and she's afraid.

The father of her first child woke up one morning eight years earlier and told her he'd booked passage on a ship to England; he left that afternoon as tears streamed down her eighteen-year-old face. *Nuh leave me,* she said. *Please, nuh leave me.* And just last year marked the end of her relationship with Cope; the squabbles, the resistance to settling down, drove her to abandon her tidy life in Montego Bay and head back to country. And yet, here is this pot-bellied charmer. She wants a partner, desperately. If she's going to be burdened, she wants someone with whom to share the struggle.

"You think you came here by accident?" George says.

She twists her mouth to one side in protest and beams at him – slightly impressed by his arrogance.

George and Dezna marry that year, 1966, and move to Pisgah. They start a family of their own, first with Maxine and then May.

In 1969, George and Dezna listen nonstop to Desmond Dekker's "Israelites" on the radio:

> *After a storm, there must be a calm*
> *They catch me in the farm*
> *You sound your alarm*
> *Poor me Israelites...*

Roddy, Carla, and Fabi are born, and the Sanderson family, as the children grow, becomes immersed in stories, particularly *Dulcimina: Her Life in Town*. It makes life in Pisgah, consumed as it is by languor among the pineapple groves, a little more interesting. The broadcast, along with Dezna's ability to run a tight ship, keeps the children out of trouble.

Originally on JBC Radio and then on Radio Jamaica Rediffusion (RJR), *Dulcimina* is dubbed a slice-of-life radio soap opera about migration within Jamaica that provides a hopeful outlook for those immersed in rural life. On Wednesdays and Thursdays at noon, Maxine, May, Roddy, Carla, and Fabi sit on the veranda overlooking the pineapple groves to listen to the fifteen-minute episodes from this Elaine Perkins radio play to block out the country's woes and descend into story-telling.

The protagonist of the radio play, Dulcimina Black, leaves her small village to make a life for herself in Western Kingston, where she stays with her cousins and an ex-con named Babes. Dulcimina takes on various challenges, but moving up in society presents more complications than she anticipates. Dezna, just like the rest of the Sanderson family, is captivated.

Though the Sandersons are strong readers and writers, Jamaica's colonial legacy had left much of the population at a supreme disadvantage, and the literacy rate at the time of independence is only about a third of the population. So for the government to communicate political agendas, the messaging appears through *Dulcimina*. It promotes a national identity and gives the assurance of strong agricultural growth. The lessons aren't exactly subtle. Dulcimina gets close to

Guided Democracy, the on-the-nose allegorical moniker of Atlas Brown, with whom she has an affair. But capitalism is dangerous, at least on the radio. Dulcimina wants jewels and other material things. She begins to worship at the altar of Mammon. The consequences for such desires in Jamaica are dire: violence and murder.

Some try to come to Dulcimina's aid such as Miss Pinny, notorious for her steamy, ongoing assignations with Dr Tacious Billet, who is dead but visits her at night through astral travels.

After all, Jamaica inspires such fantasy, because its reality is folkloric.

As the kids listen to the radio, Dezna sits at her Singer sewing machine. There are other radio plays they enjoy – *Hopeful Village*, *Raymond the Sprayman*, *Mimosa Hotel*, and *Naseberry Street*. They watch shows like *Oliver at Large*, *Titus*, and *Lime Tree Lane*. Dezna always has a big pudding pan going on the wood fireplace, and nearby she keeps a fridge for curing meats – goat tripe in particular. She often bakes Jamaican black cake. Sometimes they "run a boat", that is, cook as a group. The kids pick sorrel and shell peas. They tell Anansi stories, sing songs, listen to raindrops on the zinc roof.

In addition to her work as a seamstress and nurse, Dezna goes to New Market and sells trinkets at a higgler cart to have the family make ends meet during the country's rough period.

The CIA's economic disruption plan that Norman Descoteaux orchestrates hits pineapples hardest, deals Dezna's family a blow. Farming becomes particularly difficult, and whereas export crops like sugar, bananas, pineapple, and coffee made up almost a fifth of the GDP in the 1960s – when Dezna and Bready began their life in Pisgah with Jamaica newly independent from Britain – that percentage plummets to under a tenth during the '70s. Part of it is the CIA attack on United Fruit. The clandestine operatives in Jamaica are bigger than those in parts of Africa or elsewhere in the Caribbean at the time – and on par with the Angolan mission. These surreptitious measures are taking a toll on the island. Jamaica is becoming a dangerous place.

"Lord, have mercy," Dezna says.

The Jamaican Tourist Board reports a 30 per cent drop in American visitors from 1974 to 1976. As violence increases, Jamaica grows unsafe – even for Jamaicans. American tourists aren't going to risk it. Round Hill with its black-tie parties and Calypso bands and stush, hoity-toity guests fades in grandeur. The swinging Jamaica of the early '60s is almost unrecognizable come the mid '70s when Rohena, a full-fledged adult, decides to emigrate to America. Women, in particular, start to leave Jamaica. It's a matriarchal society ultimately, and they have to provide for their families.

Come 1980, the liberal Michael Manley is essentially ousted from office and replaced with Edward Seaga, a conservative and a capitalist.

Corporations get rich and people get poorer, all the more so as inflation skyrockets.

In a country flush with cane, families can't get sugar. If you can find it at all, the cost is prohibitively expensive. Dezna's family sweetens tea with maple syrup. Rice and peas, a Jamaican staple that typically has a low price point, becomes a luxury on Sundays. A stiff loaf of bread has to last an entire week for the ten-person Sanderson household. The family has to use milk powder. And Dezna cooks with bulgur, not regular wheat. She employs other cooking alternatives, too: bamboo dust and Muddleflush.

On Saturdays, the kids play cricket in the road. They head down to the spring to bathe and do laundry. They play hopscotch, top (which they call jig), marbles, "skip" (jump rope) and dandy shandy. Maxine leads the way for the children. Beez – Queen Beez – guides them up the main road in Pisgah and over to the drink shop for soda and an *arinj*. May skips behind. Orville and Dexter watch out for Roddy and their youngest sisters, Carla and Fabi. Cope's two boys may not get on the best with Bready – their stepfather jealously views them as a remnant of another love – but it's a motley crew whose members are unified by one unwavering force: a love for their mother. Even Winston visits Pisgah occasionally to be with Dezna but generally falls into the habit of staying at Mahogany Hill with his grandparents, rocking in a cedar chair with Maas Seamon as the man writes sermons or tells stories.

The Sanderson kids wander around the hills, the lush forests. They eat cashew fruit and avoid locus (known as stinking toe). They pick red peas (kidney beans), Jerusalem peas, pimento, black pepper. They peel the ginger they gather, and they dry it. As a reward, they drink Pip – an orange drink that destroys teeth but nourishes souls.

They are obsessed with the legend of the White Witch, a figure known to be a haunting presence at the Rose Hall Plantation in Montego Bay with its grand Georgian mansion from the 1770s whose interiors are covered in silk wallpaper decorated with palm trees and birds. A woman who comes to be known as Annie Palmer was born in Haiti, but when her English father and Irish mother die from yellow fever, a nanny adopts her and instructs her in the dark arts of voodoo and witchcraft. In 1820, when she is only seventeen, the four-eleven sparkplug comes to Jamaica and marries John Palmer, the Rose Hall Plantation owner. She has clandestine affairs with her slaves – employing the house's secret passageways – and soon thereafter murders Palmer, then two more husbands and various male slaves. But an obeah man named Takoo puts an end to her killing spree by ending her life himself after she puts a curse on his granddaughter. Carla finds this frightening. That is to say, Carla finds this riveting.

Johnny Cash's 1973 "The Ballad of Annie Palmer" helps to tell the narrative:

> *Where's your husband, Annie?*
> *Where's number two and three?*
> *Are they sleeping beneath the palms*
> *Beside the Caribbean sea?*
> *At night I hear you riding*
> *And I hear your lovers call*
> *And I still can feel your presence*
> *Around the great house at Rose Hall*

ANOTHER MOTHER

It is said that visitors can see the ghost of Annie Palmer at night riding her horse around the plantation in search of runaway slaves. Visitors to this day claim to see bloodstains or hear footsteps.

The Sanderson children are transfixed by tales – of Dulcimina, of Annie Palmer, of Mizzy at Lovers' Leap as Dezna recounts it – but come evening, they delight in another escape: ska parties. Dezna's house is the dance hall hub of Pisgah.

It's a good release for Dezna given that she's so focused on her Ministry of Health duties. Ganja is exploding in this era, and obeah and myal are still widely practised in the hills; to treat a disease, most patients still rely on magic. Sister Nurses like Dezna are travelling around to promote Western medicine – she's a New Age Granny Nanny, promoting proper methods of sanitation and safe sex. She has a vegetable scale for weighing babies on which all the children of the hills are assessed. Every other Friday, Dezna goes to Black River for a Ministry of Health conference. On Saturdays, the family goes to the Seventh-day Adventist church.

She mostly ventures the hills to treat the ill, and as the economy worsens, she comes home with yam-stuffed pockets in lieu of cash. In 1981, a father shows up at Miss Dezna's door with his daughter slung across his back. A boulder has rolled clear across her foot, crushing it. Dezna welcomes them in and puts on some water for bush tea. She cleans the wound, sterilising the breached skin and wrapping the foot. Three decades later, Maxine gets a call from the daughter looking for Miss Dezna. It is too late by a year. The hills are filled with legends of Miss Dezna and her healing powers. The most famous nurse of the Jamaican Hills will one day see a young boy in New Jersey back to health as he convalesces after a bee sting or recovers from a fractured wrist.

In Jamaica, during this busy period, she still manages to have dinner on the table for an army of ten by six o'clock. Her kids would have scarfed down dumpling and butter, but she serves escovitch fish and callaloo, curry goat, and dasheen.

A silk-cotton tree stands in the yard as a haunt for duppies, the family says. It's forty meters high at least and bursts open each year with fibrous white sheer filaments as it blooms, looming majestically over the house. The tree has a way of protecting itself, growing mace-like spikes to keep bugs and birds from eating its bark. When the trunk gets hard enough, the protection falls off, leaving a wide, strong rotundness. The Taíno used to cut these trees down to use as dugout canoes, but mostly they're left to grow for hundreds of years. They're sacred. The Sanderson children sometimes hold-hands and dance around the trunk.

Life is innocent and simple despite the difficulties. The perseverance of the family throughout the country's struggles is a testament to Dezna's tireless optimistic realism.

But in 1987, tragedy strikes.

Bready is bumping papayas down from the trees with a twelve-ounce Ting bottle rigged to a broom shaft, and Dezna is preparing a lunch of steamed red snapper.

"George?" she calls, throwing her dishrag next to the sink. "George, come yuh…"

ANOTHER MOTHER

When she gets to the nearest pineapple grove, past discarded sardine tins shining like agate, she harrumphs to herself: Bready seems to be taking a little snooze out here in the July heat instead of doing his work. Yes, Bready is taking a nap, surely, among the fallen palm fronds. *Eem lay-zy*, she thinks – almost to convince herself this is a siesta. His face is lodged in the reddish, bauxite-rich silt of the farmland.

"Georgie!"

Moments later, she feels herself call for Carla and Fabi, twelve and eleven at the time. It is important, she knows, to have left room in her heart for the unimaginable.

She realises almost immediately she can't stay here any longer. She'll have to leave the island to continue her dream and provide for her family. In a tumultuous life, she knows well enough that such tragedies are unpredictable. She has to change course.

Come September of that year, Dezna is at a loss – having built up a life that, tattered at the edges, finally tears in half. She doesn't want to tend to the pineapples; she's no farm girl. *Psh.* With her sister Rohena already in New Jersey, she decides to make a life for herself in the States.

About two hundred thousand Jamaicans like Dezna would emigrate to the United States in the 1980s, some ten per cent of the population. Maybe a robbery in Kingston, maybe a spouse's death pushed a family's solvency off a cliff. Women are pouring out of Jamaica to New Jersey, from Trenchtown to Trenton. IMF austerity measures have made the quality of life terrible on the Rock. The CIA's chokehold of the country –

lighting a match to the combustible politics – causes Jamaican women to make a change. They come to the States in droves to raise American children and care for the elderly.

Dezna has to go away and leave two growing girls behind.

"Mummy always here fi you," Dezna says. "Mummy nuh leave you."

Carla and Fabi know their lives are about to change forever. They recognise they will elevate themselves a rung into an early adulthood that requires strength and maturity. It's not a burden, though. It's just what's done. Mothers all through the hillside are leaving Jamaica. And the girls will have to make do.

14. The Nanny's Irie

The apartment is filled with the thick scent of mannish water, the stew simmering in a pot on the stove-top. I'm with Carla and Fabi at Fabi's place in Irvington, New Jersey where she lives with her two sons and husband. Carla's house, where her husband and young son have stayed for the afternoon, is just *dung di rohd*. The walls here are lilac, and the couch is a wide-wale brown corduroy.

Carla, who is five foot nothing, is the smallest of all Dezna's children, a fact that earned her the nickname Bugz. She inherited Dezna's gentleness, her calm, her tendency to dote on others – traits that serve her well as a nurse in Newark, even if she has to get help to reach items on high shelves. She also has a voice that's calming, like that of a dental hygienist. Fabi, the youngest, has Dezna's grace of movement, with a swan-like neck and demurring eyes – perhaps an elegance in keeping with her real first name, Vivienne. Her elongated face is Modigliani'd, and she is able to turn on a stern tone with her kids only the way a New Jersey public school teacher can.

I tell them about my visit with May and my time at Mahogany Hill. Their faces light up. Times were difficult, but they were pure, full of goodness. I start to ask some questions, the sort that make them shift a little on the couch. The stakes are high in the type of foreign nanny exchange our families experienced; what one boy gains in the United States, other children lose out on in the developing world.

"Was it hard when your mom left for the US?" I ask. "Did you feel short-changed on your childhood with her?"

They try to beg off any hardship at having their mother move to America when they were teenagers.

"In a sense, your mom became my mom," I say.

"But she was Mom to so many," Carla says.

Carla says she understands the important role her mother played in other people's lives as a maternal source of comfort, whether on the island of Jamaica or peninsula of New Jersey.

I tell Carla and Fabi a story about how I publicly declared myself of partially Jamaican parentage during Friday night Shabbat services at Kingston's Shaare Shalom synagogue, whose sanctuary floor is covered in white sand as an homage to when Iberian Jews, from whom many Jewmaicans are descended, prayed in secret during the Spanish Inquisition.

While I was on the bema before a congregation filled harmoniously with people of every skin palette imaginable in a distillation of Jamaica's One Love ethos, it was my turn to introduce myself and indicate my place of origin. In Judaism, it is customary to introduce yourself formally by announcing you are the son or daughter of your parents and employing their

ANOTHER MOTHER

Hebrew names. I paused, and looking out at the congregation, I wanted to introduce myself as the son of Cindy and Irv Urken and of Dezna Sanderson, but I thought that would be confusing to the audience and impossible as I didn't know any of the necessary Hebrew names.

I inhaled deeply.

"I'm Ross Kenneth Urken from Princeton, New Jersey," I said. "But Jamaica always feels like home." I heard the collective din of warm laughter throughout the sanctuary.

Yet at the Kiddush afterward, those in attendance made my Jamaican connection more secure. I suddenly was being called to the front of the reception space – "Where's Ross? Come up here," beckoned Ainsley Henriques, the paterfamilias of Jewish life in Jamaica who sounds like C-3PO and has the aspect of Q from James Bond. He's a descendant of the pirate Moses Cohen Henriques and carries a buccaneer bombast in his voice.

Now he presented me before the congregation. Calling attention to my smart suit (the one I had worn on my wedding day) and my tie, cinched in a full Windsor, he pronounced me best dressed at shul. And, he mentioned, a few nights earlier at the Liguanea Club, a stately Kingston country club featured in the opening shots of *Dr. No*, I had fit right in among the rest of Kingston society in pressed khakis and a linen shirt as white as the coconut milk that drowned the snapper on my dinner plate. Here in the synagogue, Henriques jovially explained my fashion sense: the direct result of the Jamaican nanny who raised me.

"She taught him to have a bath and *star dem threads*," he said.

The crowd roared.

Carla and Fabi chuckle at the anecdote. Dezna was always concerned with making sure her family had a bath, starched shirts, well-stitched dresses, and polished shoes.

As we sit in the living room, something that becomes more apparent for me as an adult, with Carla and Fabi in their early forties, is that they are just about ten years older than I am. I keep thinking about how much I needed Dezna as a boy and how distraught I was when she left our family after my bar mitzvah. But she left Carla and Fabi at the start of their teens, too.

After our laughter subsides, I'm still reckoning with an essential question: with Fabi and Carla, my gaining a mother certainly meant they lost one, right?

Maybe, they say, but they're inclined to think my family most needed Dezna as a saviour. Carla and Fabi also think pragmatically: this was the way the family could best survive, through Dezna's employment in the United States and the remittances she'd send home.

Of course, I feel guilt, I tell Fabi and Carla, at receiving care and affection from Dezna when they were still growing up. Dezna made a sacrifice to provide for her family, and I realise how lucky I am to have been the beneficiary of her move – blessed by the serendipitous circumstances that brought her to Hale Drive in a nor'easter. But life without their own mother while growing up? Fabi and Carla dismiss that period as A-O.K. They saw her once or twice a year during extended holiday visits, and they claim they were mature early.

ANOTHER MOTHER

"We turned out O.K.," Fabi says with a smile as we eat our mannish water.

"Wi likkle but wi Tallawah," Carla says, acknowledging their strength and, as usual, teaching me another Jamaican expression.

All the time I was in Dezna's maternal care, I was somewhat aware – but perhaps initially incurious – about the fact that she was a mother to eight others. That is not something a child may consider, but when I did start rustling the bushes for information as an adult, I became more cognizant of all she gave up.

I let Carla and Fabi know just how much their mother brought order to my home – that healing ability when I injured my wrist, her skill at breaking up parental skirmishes. But she went beyond that: she was a stabilising force at the ready who could help us all at once. One image comes to mind, I say: Dezna in the back hall with my mother after my uncle died. It requires some explaining, I tell them.

Until his curious death in a helicopter crash at the age of forty-three, Dr Todd Lewis Passoff, my mother's older brother, lived with the extravagance of one taking full advantage of his earned wealth and his God-given good looks. He had adopted his very own Camelot, created a land for a boy with his toys.

There was a fifty-foot yacht he kept by his home in Newport Beach, California. The red Ferrari Testarossa (with a coffin-sized cockpit) he'd vroom up to two hundred miles per hour. He enjoyed his Bentley Continental so much that he bought a Bentley dealership. There was the Harley and the countless other motorcycles (Triumphs, BMWs) he rode around Europe and had shipped home. He always ordered the most expensive item on the menu, whether he liked it or not. There was the mansion with, remarkably, an elevator.

He became so renowned for his neck and back surgery work, particularly involving scoliosis, that a few years after moving to California, he had opened five practices in the LA area. To travel between hospitals and avoid the traffic on the 405, he got his helicopter licence and moved efficiently between his many medical fiefdoms. Why waste forty-five minutes or an hour a couple times a day when he could hop from one helipad to the next hospital? Or so went his Icarian mindset.

That is until one fateful Friday morning: May 8, 1992.

The *Los Angeles Times* headline the next day told the story:

Doctor Dies After Crashing Copter: Surgeon Had Just Operated at Same Anaheim Hospital Before Taking Off

The article's lede further hit home the tragic irony of how a prominent orthopaedic surgeon died in the emergency room of the hospital where moments before he had – living, breathing, bantering – bettered someone else's life.

Todd had arrived early that morning at Anaheim Memorial Hospital to perform a seven-thirty knee joint replacement on a seventy-year-old patient. Once he finished the surgery, there was that pose he struck – arms crossed, rear end leaning against the ledge of the Formica counter, legs crossed at the ankles. The white surgeon's coat making his bronzed face appear all the more as if he just flew in from the Amalfi Coast.

ANOTHER MOTHER

Whistling, jiggling for the keys in his pocket, he took the elevator to the hospital's roof. He reached his private helicopter, a single-seat Robinson R22, and pulled down the collapsible blades. A less daring man might view a propeller of this ilk as flimsy, but to Todd, it was an indication of ease, that it could be operated like a toy.

It was a clear fine day in May, after all, and he was living the California dream.

He hopped in and, with a bolt, left the helipad for the sports medicine clinic he operated in Temecula – a route he had taken without fail countless times before over a four-year stretch. Todd liked to live fast, as is the reputation for orthopods, but he was a creature of precision, agility. Whether operating on a patient, or coasting by sea, road, or air in one of his toys, he brandished a cerebral exactness.

A few minutes into the flight – in a morning strung seamlessly together, churningly clockwork – something went awry.

The chopper began to wobble and veered right before spinning out of control above the Foster Sand & Gravel Co., just at the northwest corner of Patt and Commercial in Anaheim, a report would later detail. Todd grabbed the steering wheel tightly, flicked the controls desperately. There were two adjacent cylindrical levers: one throttle, the other a kill switch. For three seconds, maybe four, the craft hovered, intimating to Todd that maybe he had regained control, could come out of this one, never step back in this crummy machine, stick to the commute in cars just like everyone else.

As his mother always said: *Get rid of that thing.*

This can't be happening, he thought. *I have surgery to perform in an hour.*

Science knew how this would end: if a helicopter is above five hundred feet, it drops gradually like a twirling maple seed. At two hundred and fifty feet, which Todd achieved to get above most buildings in the area, it's a different story.

Just then the craft sputtered, pitched, and nosed straight down onto a parked pickup truck with a boom (heard over by nearby Werner Corp., a concrete company), and ricocheted onto a sand pile. It was his 15,830th day of life, his last.

Todd was thrown through the windshield of the helicopter, and those nearby who heard the crash, found him with his crisp white shirt stuck in the glass he had busted through.

Todd was unconscious with wounds to his head and chest, and emergency medical personnel took him back to Anaheim Memorial in critical condition, where physicians tried to save him – one of their own. But forty minutes later, he had failed to regain consciousness and was pronounced dead. All those forty-five-minute segments saved in the air…days, maybe weeks in aggregate. But he was left with but a half-life.

As caretaker of the house, before cell phones, Dezna got the news first. She reached my mother at my father's hardware store.

That afternoon, Dezna picked my sister and me up from the neighbourhood bus stop, and soon thereafter, when my mother came home through the back door, Dezna greeted her. My mother, carrying a teal coffee Thermos and mail, stumbled over in the back hall, and, as I watched from the threshold between the kitchen and back hall, Dezna agilely held my mother up, supported her weight.

Dezna stood there – not so much the backbone of my family, but the knees, unwavering and unwilling to give way to the g-forces life materialises to push us down.

Carla and Fabi nod, understanding. They're not exactly surprised at their mother's strength amid adversity: that is perhaps her defining characteristic.

Dezna so stressed hard work with me, and with them, because that's all she knew. To survive, you had to hustle. Jamaican joy, in all its abundance, is tinged with despair. There is a realism in Jamaica, an acknowledgment that to live is, fairly often, to suffer and endure. What good can come of life deserves gratitude. Sadness is inevitable. But mustering the strength to push through? Finding pragmatic solutions, even in less-than-ideal solutions? That takes character.

When Dezna decides to leave Jamaica in 1987, Carla and Fabi can't cry for long, can't dot their mother's dress with tears too much. She must go away to America just like Rohena. It's not that she wants to. She simply must for the sake of the family.

While Dezna is living with us in Princeton, Carla and Fabi go to a boarding high school in Cambridge in the hills of St Elizabeth and come back to Mahogany Hill for weekends with Orville and his then girlfriend.

Carla and Fabi will spend their teenage years without their mother around, and their impression of Dezna's life during that time – of the stories from Princeton, from America in general, and of the two new children their mother is raising – comes during Dezna's biannual visits for Christmas and Easter. They hear stories of Nicole and Ross, of well-meaning parents who are constantly at loggerheads, of neighbourhood walks around Hale Drive kicking crab apples into gutters.

There's no self-pity in their sentiment about the time. They stay strong. You can't control everything that happens to you in the world, but you can control your reaction.

"We run tings," Fabi says. "Tings nuh run we."

15. The Society of Jamaican Nanny Boys

It's spring, almost a year after I started calling Rohena and soon after meeting May in Florida, and I'm sitting with Orville and his wife, Ivy, in the Olympic Flame Diner on Amsterdam Avenue in the Lincoln Square neighbourhood of Manhattan, waiting for Rohena and her husband, Frank, to arrive.

It has taken some doing to get Rohena to agree to meet. She spends most of her time in Jamaica between Kingston and Spanish Town these days. Frank, who has been a New York City yellow-cab driver for forty years, still works most of the year up here, and Rohena has joined for a couple months in Brooklyn.

The couple had gone to church in Manhattan that morning, and this is a convenient waypoint to have a meal before heading home.

Though I've never seen Rohena in my life, not even a picture, I know it's her immediately when I spy her through the diner window coming down the block.

"Oh, there she is," I say.

"You know, because you see Dezna, don't you?" says Ivy, who usually has a tough, no-nonsense tone gained from her job as a bus driver for NJ Transit, where she met Orville. Here, she's softer. She knows how important this moment is.

And she's spot on. Had I not planned this brunch and instead just passed this woman randomly on the street, I would have believed I was hallucinating and seeing my dear nanny walking across West Sixty-first Street.

Rohena has Dezna's face and her style. In fact, her black dress with white polka dots is a near replica of the one Dezna would wear when I was growing up. She has on taupe high heels, and her hair, slightly greyed, has the elegant fullness that only morning-of curlers can provide. She has on Coke-bottle glasses, and Frank jumps ahead of her to get the door. She has an amused pertness to her smile that belies just a smidge of shyness.

We gesture over to them as they stop by the hostess stand, and in a matter of seconds, I am hugging this near twin of Dezna's – a little taller, with slightly bigger polka dots on her dress, but a person with the same energy.

"Hello, Ras," she says, pulling back to look at me.

Frank, in a linen shirt with a large Zion Lion pendant necklace and a straw hat, looks like he might be a dub music producer about to drop a diss track. He shakes my hand and does the Rasta handshake that resembles an abbreviated thumb war.

ANOTHER MOTHER

We take our seats and go around the table ordering eggs, toast, bacon. When it's Rohena's turn, she pauses – slightly overwhelmed by the variety of options.

"I beg your pardon," she says, the way Dezna would have, an overly apologetic British tendency. She orders her eggs scrambled, then over easy, then changes back to scrambled. She gets a black tea, and when it comes, she sprinkles a little salt in it just as Dezna used to do. "It's good for the system," she says.

We talk about life in Mahogany Hill, how much Dezna cared for everyone, especially when she moved back from Montego Bay. She was cooking, changing diapers, picking gungo peas, scrubbing pots, studying to be a nurse.

"I don't know how she did it," Rohena says.

We discuss the stories, the ones of Granny Nanny, of Lovers' Leap. The way the forest smells there among the pineapple groves that grow expansively into the gully. We marvel at the way peeny-wallies fly and at how industrious Dragon can be. And, of course, we talk about Junior.

"Him a rudebwoy," Frank says.

At the end of the meal as we're talking and drinking the last of our coffee and tea, Frank nudges Rohena.

"He look like Max," he says to her, pointing at my face.

Max, I think. My father begged to name me Max, but my mother's original choice won out. I'm thinking, somehow, they know this information from Dezna and that my would-be name maybe more appropriately fits my appearance.

"Max – Max is the little boy I nannied," Rohena says.

"Oh," I said. "I didn't realise…"

I knew Rohena had worked as a nurse for a period in the States, but I never know about her other career. It turns out, she fell in working for a prominent family on the Upper East Side with two girls. And when the father remarried another woman and had a son, she watched after this new child. She'd return to Jamaica, Queens with Frank on the weekends – or head out to East Hampton with the family – and later Frank and she moved to West Orange, where Dezna would spend weekends with them.

"He look exactly like Max," Frank marvels.

Rohena blushes.

"Well, maybe I should grab a drink with him," I say.

They tell me his last name, and because they talk with him via phone, they don't have his email address. I'm sure I can dig it up, I tell them.

When we're leaving the diner to return to their car, Rohena wants to take a cab the fifteen blocks. She's wearing heels, after all. But Frank, a hack himself, thinks taking a taxi that distance is an indulgence. She playfully puts up her dukes in a why-I-oughtta invitation for fisticuffs. A second later they burst out in laughter.

Then they walk hand in hand up Amsterdam Avenue.

Rohena gives a little half-turn around, just the upper part of her body.

"Have fun with Max," she says as she continues her journey north.

***

ANOTHER MOTHER

Not long after on an early evening with just a hint of chill in the air, I walk into Miss Lily's, a Jamaican restaurant in Manhattan's SoHo neighbourhood, to meet Max and also Johnny, Max's childhood friend whose nanny, Bernice, befriended Rohena. Buju Banton reggae blasts from speakers, and neon lights cascade across the interiors from wall mirrors to booths.

They're already at the bar, and though they are four years younger than I am, they seem older somehow, more established with their crisp dry-cleaned white shirts and law degrees. They stand from their stools to shake hands, and the mere handshakes have the twisting encore where the horizontal initial position turns to become a vertical "What up, man?" gesture.

Max, indeed, resembles me, if slightly taller and better looking.

Our rendezvous here had taken some logistical teeth-pulling. After my brunch with Rohena, I'd dug up Max's work email in a Google search and shot him a note to explain my journey to understand Dezna's life and desire to get more insight into the nanny-child relationship from someone who had a similar experience. He was on vacation and travelling for work, but he articulated how important the nanny bond is and seemed to understand why I might want to meet to chat as part of my quest.

Max and Johnny, they explain, have been friends since they were in diapers on the Upper East Side, and they went on to New York City's private schools and the Ivy League together. But in the bar as we sip on Red Stripes, they immediately accept me as one of the group because of our shared connection. We are something of the Society of Jamaican Nanny Boys, appreciative of our mentors' influence and carrying their legacy like a portable conscience in every action. We have no charter or escutcheon. But all our nannies got a candle of honour at our bar mitzvahs.

In the divorce from his first wife, Max's father said his ex-wife could keep the house. He just wanted to make sure Rohena would come and help raise Max, the son he would have with his new wife.

In the bar, we reminisce about how our nannies yelled at characters on the TV, during daily soaps, talk shows like *Maury* and *Ricki Lake*, and sitcoms like *Living Single* and *Martin*. Max says he heard that when his older half-sister couldn't sleep as a kid, she crawled into bed with Rohena to watch *Roots*. Bernice and Rohena were news hounds, much like Dezna, Max and Johnny tell me. They had elaborate opinions and encouraged debate with us boys over breakfast: kitchen counter intelligence. The O.J. Simpson trial, Operation Desert Storm, Bill Clinton's impeachment process – they pontificated on the issues and entered into adult dialogue with us. Each morning, Dezna described particular politicians as "shttoopid" and mentioned various "isss-yoos" she had with events around the globe as she scrunched her nose. It's perhaps no surprise Max and Johnny became lawyers and I a journalist.

As the two boys would play in the park during their childhood, Bernice and Rohena would chat, bond. The two boys grew up like brothers. The definition of family is porous and I

ANOTHER MOTHER

suggest to Max that we're practically cousins, the sons of sisters Rohena and Dezna. He laughs and accepts the comparison, if taking it with a grain of salt.

The thing is, Max and Johnny don't necessarily view Rohena or Bernice as second mothers. They both view their nanny as an important relative in their house and force in their upbringing. In the case of Max, Rohena was more of an in-house aunt who was extra hands-on but wasn't necessarily double-cast with his actual mom. For Johnny, given that Bernice was older and is now a nonagenarian, he always thought of her as more of a grandmother figure.

I'm also curious whether their upbringing lent them an affinity for Jamaica as mine did. I tell them about my travels in Mahogany Hill, my consumption of jackfruit and jellies, my banter with Dragon and Junior.

"Well, I've been to Jamaica," Max says. "But not like that..."

He went on a trip with his girlfriend and stayed at Half Moon in Montego Bay. He enjoyed the vibe of Jamaica but didn't really explore beyond the resort. It had been a warm getaway during the winter.

Johnny gives this some thought while jabbing his tongue at his bicuspid as if trying to dislodge a popcorn kernel. He says he's never been to Jamaica, but his big affinity for the island's culture stems from its food.

In fact, he meets up with Bernice once a month at his parents' apartment in the city. They catch up as they cook johnnycake, doughy festival, fried fish, fried plantains, rice and peas. He updates her on his career and his relationship with his girlfriend. Once they sit down for the meal together, she asks after Max and then tells him she's already heard this or that piece of news from Rohena. She recently had a blowout ninetieth birthday party in Brooklyn, and Johnny went with his girlfriend.

Max sees Rohena semi-regularly on holidays and special family occasions, but less frequently, because Rohena spends most of her time in Jamaica.

Upon hearing all this, I'm stung with sorrow. Rohena and Bernice would likely be there when these guys get married. They'll hold their cooing children. They're there on the phone when these two need to touch home base or get an opinion on a family issue. If only Dezna could have lived far into her dotage, we could have, for decades, walked the hills of St Elizabeth, picking and eating mangoes along the way. We could have strolled through Central Park and kicked acorns and crab apples like old times. We would have danced at my wedding, a special dance – for another mother of the groom. Dezna would have held my future son or daughter.

"You guys are lucky," I say.

They sense my sadness and nod.

"It's a special kind of relationship," Johnny says.

Of course, not everything was always hunky-dory in our nannies' lives as they brought us up. West Orange was a home base, a nexus between Dezna's travel to Princeton and Rohena's into New York City. It also became a point of neutralisation, where our nannies could deal with the struggles they faced in private. A humble apartment between Park Avenue and

Princeton's Hale Drive, it was a secret refuge that offered a lens into where these women came from. Max clued me into the fact that Dezna's life could be dramatic when she lived with Rohena.

In one instance in the mid-1990s, Rohena's husband, Frank, was stabbed and robbed while driving his taxi in Manhattan. He didn't know what to do, so he pulled up to the Park Avenue building where Max's family lived. The doorman called up to Max's father, who rushed down with Rohena to help Frank who was bleeding from his back through his shirt. They got him to nearby Lenox Hill Hospital for treatment. Though Dezna, Rohena, and Frank left Jamaica in part to escape the rampant violence occurring there, they came face-to-face with it stateside.

Frank returned to West Orange to recover, and Dezna would use her knowledge of nursing to change his bandages and dress his wounds during the weekend when she was home.

My sister and I heard nothing of it. We only knew calm nights of *Jeopardy!* with Dezna on Hale Drive amid the lamppost-lit lindens. That's because the Dinky separated her life within our home from her life without in a tidy fashion. It was a gateway to a getaway.

The Dinky has long had the shortest regularly scheduled rail route in the country – a 2.8-mile track during my childhood between the Princeton University campus and Princeton Junction for connections to New York and Trenton. The route is getting shorter and shorter too as the Princeton stop moves farther away from Nassau Street, the town's main drag. For more than 140 years, the celebrated train has brought famous scholars, statesmen, and writers to the University and actors to the nearby McCarter Theatre. It was Einstein's portal to New York and long shuttled Noble Prize-winner John Nash for his daily ride from home to the office.

It was also Dezna's vehicle in and out of Princeton, connecting her to Princeton Junction and on to the rest of New Jersey – a life I never saw.

The Dinky is a quintessential part of an old-timey Ivy League tradition and seeps into the town's character like clove cigarette smoke into a tweed ulster.

In my childhood, we'd drop Dezna off there, and she'd stand among the professors heading back to their TriBeCa lofts and students going to spend a night in Manhattan. Like at the Hale Drive school bus stop, she stood out in contrast to the rest of the crowd.

The Dinky holds a special place in my heart – the familiar musk of old intellectuals, the drab plastick-y brown leather of the seats, the unspoken decorum of recognising a famous person and nodding but not being too officious, the sticky linoleum of the floor. From my childhood bedroom just past the Princeton Battlefield as Dezna tucked me in, I would hear the spirited toot of the Dinky as I drifted off to sleep, a resonant lullaby that played harmony to her own song.

Sure, from the Dinky's vantage point across University Place, the sunlight celebrates the imposing neo-Gothic architecture. But mostly what I think of when considering the Dinky is Dezna, immersed in this societal stratification, these put-on airs in this squished social petri dish in which she had no interest. She cared not about her station in life, particularly when travelling from Princeton to West Orange.

There is sentimental value in this little one-car train that is all caboose and nothing else. This is the train where we would leave Dezna to go to another world, a portal to another universe. I can see Dezna still at that stop in her overcoat heading out of our world and transporting herself to another. It is the train where I picked up Dezna that final Thanksgiving together. When I visit Princeton these days, the ring of the divine Dinky bell makes me wonder about the other side.

The Dinky had long held a veil to the part of New Jersey that was some nethersphere between Princeton and New York City, a vortex I was only now unearthing. Though Dezna was with my family those years, I never really knew the strife she dealt with, the difficulties her kids went through to make it here. Max and Johnny know too well that we didn't see the whole story of an emotionally loaded past. Our nannies simply lavished us with love. The life that existed beyond, past the Dinky tracks or on the other side of the Hudson, was mysterious, as was the life up twisting dirt roads in the hills of St Elizabeth. But that Dezna, Rohena, and Bernice endured confirmed their resoluteness – impressive and unwavering.

Max, Johnny, and I slug the last of our Red Stripes and head outside, where night has fallen. The two have separate dinners to get to. We shake hands and part ways. I'd be off to the Upper West Side where I make extra money tutoring the kids of a wealthy Jamaican family. When I first moved to the city we'd randomly been connected, and I'd become a worker for them in Brooklyn and now their new abode. The doorman sends me up, and the kids and I work on essays and read aloud from newspaper articles with vocabulary words I make them write down just as Dezna made me do.

"Blessings," I turn and say. Max and Johnny smile, even if they're a little confused.

"See you, man," Max says.

16. The Aftermath

I have spent extensive time with seven of Dezna's eight children; I've just never met Roddy, though he lives nearby in New Jersey. Winston, Orville, Dexter, Maxine, May, Carla, and Fabi have all made the effort to form a close relationship with me. We meet up a couple times a year and all text frequently with birthday messages, old photos we've come across, life updates, heart emojis. Dexter tends to sign off with "Nuff love".

And though I've met his daughter, Ronique, at family get-togethers, Roddy has always remained elusive. He recently hit a rough patch in his personal life and wasn't necessarily in the mood for visits. And as part of the hustle endemic to the Jamaican sensibility, he's also always busy working at a grocery store and tackling other side jobs. He's a tad shyer than his brothers and values his alone time. After all, he's the only son of George and Dezna, right smack in the middle of his four sisters in terms of birth order, and thus has long sought some solitude away from a busy family.

I did finally schedule a breakfast with Roddy on a Saturday before his shift at work, but when I drove down to Linden, he was a no-show. Instead I texted Orville, and the two of us went to a Jamaican breakfast place nearby for cornmeal porridge and ackee and saltfish. Then someone called his cell, and I thought maybe Roddy had changed his mind.

"That was Broddy," Orville said, putting his phone back in his pocket after a quick back and forth.

"Roddy?"

"No, a friend of mine named Broddy."

Womp, womp.

Whereas Dezna's other children have embraced me as a sibling, Roddy has kept his distance. And that is perfectly all right. Maybe he feels indifferent towards our shared connection through Dezna. Maybe we'll find time in the future to connect. Maybe we won't. Of course, his reluctance to get together brings into relief the enthusiasm Dezna's other children have had in forming a bond. I do not take for granted their willingness to forge relationships with me, nor do I begrudge Roddy his decision.

During our Jamaican breakfast, Orville tells me that when he was thirty-three in 1995, the year of the bank bailout in Jamaica, he moved to New Jersey and lived with his mother in West Orange, while she worked for my family during the week. Jamaica wasn't a sustainable place for a young man to make a living and raise a family. That paved the way for the rest of the siblings, besides Beez, to come to the United States. Soon after Orville arrived, Dezna was treating Frank's stab wounds. She presented Orville with the harsh reality of what could happen even to those working hard to make something of themselves in their adopted homeland.

Sometimes in West Orange, Dezna slept on a mattress on a floor, its sheetless surface stained with sepia sweat rings. Sometimes she slept on the floor itself. But at that time, Nicole and I never knew of that life outside of her pink coral carpeted room with the TV and Singer sewing machine.

Orville began working for NJ Transit in 1999, driving a bus. When Dezna would return home on weekends to West Orange, Orville said he would get quite the impression of my family's life – my parents' fights, my obsession with johnnycake. While I lived a life of affection and learning and saw only the dynamic of our house, Dezna's whole family had a gaze into the Urkens' life – a one-way mirror. Orville was able to hold that perspective while maintaining insight into Dezna's struggles, her yearning for her homeland, her endurance of the losses she faced in life.

For so long, Dezna, our household's scald protector, helped keep the Urkens safe. And then we grew up.

In particular, I became a man, at least by the statutes of Jewish law. That is, I became a bar mitzvah, and this milestone doubled as a ceremony to say goodbye to Dezna on behalf of our household. Dezna, of course, would be part of the candle-lighting ceremony at Green Acres. This rite, where a person or multiple people are honoured to illuminate each of the thirteen candles with the bar mitzvah boy, was an embarrassing execution of poorly metered ABAB rhyming stanzas – oh-noetry at its worst.

Green Acres Country Club – what a place. We belonged to this Jewish golf establishment in Lawrenceville, New Jersey, mostly because my mother thought it would be a nice place to throw my bar mitzvah reception. Every time my father pulled into the club, he would sing the theme song to the 1960s sitcom that shared its name with the club's:

Green Acres is the place to be

Farm livin' is the life for me

Some may have viewed this as exceedingly corny, but this was a hardware shop owner who now belonged to a members-only establishment. Give him that indulgence.

In the ballroom when it was Dezna's turn to come up and light the candle dedicated to her and her help in raising me, she meekly walked forth before the crowd, scrunching up her mouth to her nose; she hated to be before an audience. I pulled her in by my side to pose for the photographer, and though she would no longer live with us going forward, I knew she would always be a part of my family.

Still, Dezna was around now and again, even though she moved on to another household.

When I was a junior in high school and my parents went on vacation to Mexico, Dezna spent a long weekend with us. I had an indoor track meet at school that Saturday, so Nicole, who had taken a gap year before Harvard and was just back from Spain, drove us all to Lawrenceville's field house. I suffered from panic attacks over the stress of desired academic perfection and spent many evenings breathing into a brown lunch bag, tasting the gritty paper as it became moist with my

ANOTHER MOTHER

exhalations. In class, I would lean my chair back and then press the front two wooden legs onto my feet to feel the distracting pain in a way that helped me regulate my breath. Running became the antidote, trekking with the distance runners in a five-mile loop around the neighbourhoods that surrounded campus and out towards I-95, by Green Acres, stomping on the snow or crickle-creek ice spilling over to the road pull-off zone – we in T-shirts and shorts, maybe thin gloves and skullcaps. I swallowed air, pumped my quads, learned to tolerate pain in order to endure my brain's changing chemistry.

All that preparation came to a head with Dezna watching me in the second heat of the mile. I was not on the level of the elite runners who ran 4:30 flat. I had a consistent 5:30 pace, give or take a few seconds. In an awkward uniform – the shorts leaving little to the imagination, the tank top putting my chicken-wing shoulder blades on full display – I took my mark and glanced over at Dezna, waiting for the crack of the ref's gun.

I shot out towards the front of the pack and trailed two runners as I hugged the inside lane. Because this was a small two-hundred-meter indoor track – with eight laps for a mile – my strategy was not to make too much of a major move until the fourth lap. Earlier, and I'd risk running on empty. Later, and there wouldn't be enough time to catch the leaders during their kick. Dezna was watching, and I had to turn it up.

At the fourth lap, I passed the second-place runner and felt the momentum a few seconds later to pump ahead of the first-place guy to take the lead.

Oh, shit, I thought. I had to finish this race strong.

In my peripheral vision, I'd see Dezna cheering and felt my legs launch forward even though I desperately needed reprieve. I had gone anaerobic, hoping my body would recover enough while in motion to sustain this pace. My arms flailed, and in my uncoordinated scamper with my shorts pulled high, I was more Urkel than Urken.

The world was a blur – the crowd fading in chaos like the brushstrokes in a Leroy Neiman painting – and I heard the final lap bell ring. I started to feel nauseous and looked back over my shoulder to judge whether my competition was gaining on me and saw the second-place runner some fifty metres back. My coach scolded me not to turn around, screamed at me just to finish strong.

"Run, mon," Dezna shouted.

I zipped around that final two-hundred-metre loop as if slowing down meant I'd take a bullet to my head. Sweat poured into my eyes, my quads burned, and the discs in my lower back tolerated the impact of my finishing lope. I won the race, crossing the finish at five minutes and thirteen seconds, what would be my fastest-ever mile.

Off to the side, I gave my sister and Dezna light hugs – so as not to sweat on them – and took a swig of orange Gatorade.

In front of Dezna – *for* Dezna – I overextended the limits of my physical abilities, my legs obeying the prodding of my mind. My body could not process the exertion, nor could it the liquid. I ran out of the field house to the parking lot, where I vomited the Gatorade in visceral wretches.

This was the one race of mine Dezna attended – the only I've ever won.

Of course, as a family, we saw Dezna less frequently over the years, as she had commitments with a new family and her own. Sometimes, though, she'd pay a visit to our house in Princeton with Carla. My mom would put on Bob Marley's *Legend*.

But as I prepared to go to college, things unravelled for my parents. Dezna had been our family's anchor, an anchor in drywall. And the more screwed-up my family became, the more securely she stood to hold us in place. With the kids around less and no Dezna to intervene, to modulate, to temper, my parents couldn't sustain their relationship. The strain that she had helped to keep at bay snapped the foundation of their marriage.

Partly because of her absence, my parents divorced shortly before I went to college. I was seventeen and the only kid at home, my sister off at college. I packed up my childhood bedroom – paperbacks, snow globes, the buffalo nickel, Hammer's key, the Jamaican coin-filled piggy bank with a Bustamante one-dollar bill on top – into crenellated cardboard boxes in honour of their ruptials and, my bangs drooping in teenage whimsy, transferred my status from day to boarding student at Lawrenceville.

My family put its Hale Drive house in the cul-de-sac on the market – the one Dezna had tidied and held together. My father moved to a dingy apartment, my mother into a townhouse. My parents had a civil divorce and then a Jewish one. At school, I lived in a house with six other seniors.

Dezna, for me, was always a sounding board. As my family broke apart, Dezna was a voice on the phone unfading. After she left our house, I called on her to check in – her birthday, Christmas, and Easter – but I had immersed myself in my studies in high school and then college. She was busy raising the new set of kids, and I was preoccupied trying to do her proud.

From Princeton's campus, I was heading into job interviews in the city and searching for an apartment, a new life after graduation – all from the Dinky.

I'd call Dezna to seek her counsel, commiserate about rejections, and receive validation from her pride in my triumphs. She screamed through the phone with excitement when I told her I'd mostly overcome my fear of flying by working with a shrink who had me sit for six hours at Newark Liberty International Airport to watch planes take off like clockwork without any trouble. In part, viewing giddy Americans blithely jetting off to Paris, Buenos Aires, and Montego Bay instilled in me an anger that I was not able to take part in that adventurous spirit despite my desire to see the world. But what really pushed me onto the tarmac in years to come?

"There's nothing to fear, Ras-mon," Dezna said through the phone. I'd hear those words every time I sat with sweaty palms before boarding.

As for my parents, perhaps in character for them, in indecision and neurosis, they managed to find their way back to each other.

A Jewish marriage tradition has the groom stomp on a glass to remember, even in joy, the destruction of the Second Temple of Jerusalem and the shattering sorrows of life. Of course, the old quip indicates this is the last time a groom gets to put his foot down (true for my father, who used a halogen bulb from the store for dramatic breakage). But mystical Judaism offers a retrieval of happiness in the midst of this wreckage: the Jewish concept of *tikkun olam* ("repairing the world") holds that God extracted part of his essence into containers of light when creating the world, and in a smashing of vessels similar to the wedding glass, these shards are considered light held within the material of creation. Despite demolition, it is possible to reunite these fragments in repair.

The spring before Dezna died in 2010, my divorced parents had their second wedding – twenty-eight years after their original wedding day. All told, their relationship arithmetic traces the route of an irregular cardiogram: three months of courtship, twenty-two years of marriage, four years of divorce (during which my father briefly married another woman), two years of dating each other again. Then that beautiful, strangely soap-operatic turn.

During a college summer I had spent in France in 2007, my mother confessed to me by telephone (amid gossipy gum-chewing pops) that she and my father had reconnected. She whispered the news giddily as if to one of her girlfriends at lunch.

"Dad and I have started to…go out again," she said, her voice jumping a dozen decibels.

"Citizens of Aix-en-Provence," I wanted to scream, "my parents may be going steady!"

In all earnestness, I was thrilled but maintained a degree of scepticism. After all, I was dealing with a *Mater hebraeica*, who explained that her biggest problem with my father now proved taxonomical: how to classify each other socially.

"So what do you call yourselves?" I wondered in clinical disbelief.

"Dad introduces me as his 'ex-ex-wife,'" she said. And then as if that weren't enough: "You should see the looks we get!"

My mother delighted in the awkwardness; we come, indeed, from a strange breed of emotional masochists. At the very least, my parents agreed to be "happily divorced".

Because precisely labelling them — "ex-ex-spouses" or "boyfriend and girlfriend" – was ultimately impossible, perhaps in the age of Facebook, pithiness would group them under "It's Complicated". Such was the title of that Alec Baldwin/Meryl Streep flick released at the time about a man rekindling a relationship with his ex-wife. The tagline: "Divorced... with benefits".

A year after my parents had split, my father met another woman. My mother got professional headshots and took to the uncertain pastures of JDate. She suffered a number of bad Internet set-ups (decrying the pool "slim pickins") and had a *Sex and the City*-esque group of divorcées who drove to Meatpacking District clubs: think dish sessions and stilettos. My sister took the brunt of Mom's lonely calls when even marital mediocrity stood preferable to solitude.

My parents stayed connected throughout their divorce, taking demonstrative pride in the prestigious educations of their two children – bumper stickers, sweatshirts. They'd meet at parents' weekends, talk tuition and logistical matters.

When the reconciliation began I still do not know exactly: my father started to bring flowers and, at some point, moved into the townhouse. Such stories cannot be chronicled precisely, placed in a system of causes and effects, but their re-love seems to have had the same onset pattern as sleep: gradually and then all at once. My parents had enough history to weather the craziness of divorce and explore the possibility of a relationship once again.

Emotional history does not go away, after all. It's relentless.

In the face of the "it's complicated" status my parents faced in their second go at marriage, they fearlessly moved forward. In demolishing their collective vessel – the shards painful, the original destroyed – they were able to create something else luminescent in rebuilding.

Even in her absence, my parents have acknowledged that Dezna served as a source of reason in their arguments – all those years she talked them down from the ledge still yielding dividends in how they managed their behaviour.

My immediate family seemed to be repaired – Cindy and Irv standing in their front yard, almost comically intrepid to give it another go.

But Dezna, whom I'd had last seen the previous Thanksgiving, was notably absent at my parents' re-wedding and missed seeing my father look like he was in a "Buy 1, Get 3" Jos. A. Bank print ad. Dezna was moving more slowly those days, couldn't make it – weaker in her late sixties than she might have been had diabetes not taken its toll. She was having loss of vision and suffered bouts of low energy.

Then that fall, her daughter Carla called.

"You've got to come," she said.

My sister and I had taken the train to Newark Penn Station that day and livery-cabbed it to the hospital. Amid the rusty container ports through the window and drab brick flickering by – autumn all around us – I flashed back. Kicking crab apples on a walk with Dezna up to the upper portion of our development, calves pumping to keep up with her swift pace – she'd walked hills greater than this, she'd say. Dezna waiting to pick us up from the bus stop and walk home with us there on Hale Drive – she, in her regular brown house skirt and a black top amid all the other white mothers in the neighbourhood. Dezna's invitation to *come, let's have some tea*. Dezna shyly walking up in front of two hundred people to light an honorary candle at my bar mitzvah. Dezna laughing uproariously every time Joe Pesci eats it throughout *Home Alone*.

Dezna had been sleeping when we walked into the hospital room, and she stirred awake in those white hospital sheets. She beamed her wise eyes at us – once again this little trinity reunited, like when we used to say our prayers in the Creamsicle-lit room.

We gave her mini life-updates: relationships, careers. I told Dezna I was dating a bohemian musical theatre actress from Oklahoma. I explained how my mother had tried to stop Tiffan and me from moving in together; in a last-ditch effort she had chased us down the sidewalk to try to prevent Tiffan from taking away her baby boy. Tiffan, with straw-blond hair and green eyes, intimidated my mother. That she acted in plays with *Seinfeld*'s Jason Alexander and Tovah Feldshuh did not quite earn her the Semitic street cred my mother craved in a daughter-in-law. Two policemen had to intervene as my mother ran after Tiffan down Ninth Avenue, I told Dezna. Certainly, in the way I sought some distance from my mother in my relationship with Dezna, so too did I with my choice in a romantic partner.

Still, Dezna said I had to respect my mother, care for her always.

"I know," I said.

All I knew of hospital bedside visits I learned watching *General Hospital* with Dezna. I did not know how to behave here. Should I be chipper to cheer her up? I held her hand and smiled. I sought to care for her and nourish her with the Kozy-Shack rice pudding. She uhm-uhmed at the sweetness.

Ultimately, the Caribbean churchwomen entered the room, shuffled, murmured, shuffled some more. They told her that she was soon heading to paradise, out of this earthly pain. They called her Sister Sanderson.

The rest of our stay they Sister Sanderson'd her and sang boisterously and loved on her. But those moments, those few precious moments of her extra children by her bed holding hands, those were gone. There in some drab wing of a health facility – the fetid stench blending with the ammonia – lay someone to whom I owed everything. She drifted off to sleep.

The Aftermath

The next weekend Tiffan took the train with me to Newark, where Dezna had been moved to hospice. Carla and her husband, Vinnie, picked us up and drove us to see Dezna.

When Tiffan and I entered the room, Dezna was fast asleep. I grabbed her hand. Could she feel me? *Please.*

Now that I was old enough, I had so many questions to ask about how she summoned such strength in her life. She still had so much wisdom to impart. I pled silently.

O.K., I'll write my name. I'll write my name.

Right then, when I most needed her insights, she was unavailable. She was in a deep slumber and would not wake up that afternoon – her body was resting, fighting to recover, but she was on her way to leaving this world slowly. Tiffan sang to Dezna, and I held her hand as Carla looked on.

Promise, I'll write my name. Swear it. I'll write my name. Big R.

But there would be no more asking Dezna questions, no more bobsled back to my room.

Please, let me write my name. Anything.

A week later, I would get the call from Carla.

I confronted the future with the largesse of Dezna's lessons, but I wasn't fully ready to move on. I still needed to connect with her. And since the future was no longer, I had no recourse but to look to the past.

Tiffan and I would get married two years later, and her charge from her nannying days in the Hamptons served as our ringbearer. We teased Luke, who had nannies from Poland and other parts of Europe, about the time he asked Tiffan, "So what language do they speak in Oklahoma?"

ANOTHER MOTHER

As the years passed, the Urkens continued to evolve. But of course: *plus ça change*. My parents moved into a new house in a fifty-five-and-older community on the outskirts of Princeton, and my mother decked out their abode in her own collection of Hunter Douglas venetian blinds and tufted ottomans. The man who bought my father's hardware store building opened a shop called Holsome Teas & Herbs, which sells holistic remedies and hosts yoga and Zen meditation classes.

It is difficult to cultivate previous glory, though. In my grandfather's old tomato fields, it is said, the soil is arid now. The farmers, instead, grow potatoes. As empty nesters, newly reunited, my parents ultimately saw their second-time-around honeymoon phase dissolve. My father started sleeping upstairs, my mother in the first-floor bedroom. My mother yelled, and my father fired back dismissive ripostes in his quip-pro-quo style. They blew up at each other so frequently that they just stopped talking to each other altogether. Dezna was not there to intervene with a "Cho!" or hold a family meeting.

My father began to drink on the sly again. I would never fully understand the answers he was looking for in the bottom of those bottles.

Left to their own devices, my parents approached their seventies by sabotaging their newfound romance. They recently finalised their second divorce.

"Wait, that's a thing?" a friend recently said upon hearing the news.

Nicole, who is now a mother, and her husband, Jordan, raise their son, Dylan, with the help of a Trinidadian nanny named

The Aftermath

Kathy Ann. When I watch Dylan play with his nanny and she calls him so sweetly in her own Trini sing-song, my eyes well up with tears.

"Deee-lahn," she says.

He has no idea how lucky he is to be experiencing these moments.

17. One Blood

Coco, Maxine's husband, is driving us down the road in a shuttle, and I'm entrusted with holding Dezna's tombstone on my lap. We picked it up the previous day from Sam Isaacs & Son Funeral Home, just across from 39 Market Street in Montego Bay, where Dezna and Cope once lived, where she had come to meet him for the first time that one morning in 1960, where she had laid eyes on this veritable giant who smelled of Craven "A" cigarettes, where she had scroonched up her nose at the offer of a Red Stripe. It was here that she had wandered in ballet flats down to Sam Sharpe Square – her lungs filled with promise in this new city.

It is Easter Monday, and we're zooming to Pisgah through Queen of Spain Valley to lay Dezna's headstone at her pink-tiled grave next to Bready's blue-tiled one. Orville, Ivy, and their son, Cory; May, Desmond, and Diamond; Maxine, Coco, and their children, twenty-two-year-old Jellicia (Jelli) and Blue-Blue, now twelve; and I buckle up for the two-hour journey around switchbacks and into the hills of St Elizabeth, then still higher than the village of Mahogany Hill where I'd once travelled with Dragon. We've packed into coolers fish wrapped in foil, Red Stripes, yams, bottled water, and kick-down for a feast.

The whole way to Pisgah as the shuttle shakes under the bumps of unpaved roads and stops short around blind turns, my quads strain to hold up Dezna's heavy headstone.

When we pull up to the old Sanderson homestead, Dexter is waiting by the road with a wide grin, and Queen is there with Junior, who is smoking a bionic skunk fatty.

"Weh yuh deh pon?" I say.

"All fruits ripe, mon," Junior says.

Behind Junior, there is a stately panna cotta-coloured stucco and wood house with a sizable veranda overlooking the pineapple groves. In the distance, lumpy green hills rise along the horizon, and we bring the food down stone steps to a fold-up table on a cement patio. On a slope burns a tidy campfire that will cook the fish.

Suppose one day you will visit me there...

A small group of villagers has assembled to feast, celebrate, and honour Dezna. A steep dirt hill with patchy grass leads from the road to the gravesite and other family shrines. I hold Diamond's hand as we walk down, the ground littered with sardine tins.

"There's Rasta, your namesake," Orville says with a smile as he indicates a relative's tomb.

A bunch of men are standing around drinking Red Stripes and kick-down, and out of the huddle emerges Dragon as the men, all at least a clear foot taller than him, make way for this guy with all of his swagger.

"Wah gwaaaan?" he says, giving me the Rasta thumb war handshake.

"Wah gwaan?" I say.

"Bless up," he says, raising his glass in a toast. "Nuff love."

Dragon will eventually be tasked with using a saw to carve into the grave tiles and make a cut-out square for the tombstone. He ambles up the hill to get organised.

I walk to where Dezna is buried, next to her husband, in an intricately tiled seashell-pink grave. I take the time to put my hands on the smooth tomb, feel the ceramic on my fingertips, press my love into the stone. Dezna has made it full circle back to her island, and I think about the sacrifices she made and the hardships she endured in her life, from Mahogany Hill, to Montego Bay, to Pisgah, to West Orange, to Princeton, to Newark, and back to Pisgah. At her grave, I silently communicate my gratitude. She gave so much to her children, including me, throughout her life and has left a combined, hybrid family in her wake. I am accepted as a sibling among her children, an uncle to her grandchildren. I went just in search of her, and I found an entirely new family in the process.

I linger here with Dezna like the old days, at the TV at night or mornings during her breakfast table musings (we were the early risers) before heading to the bus stop. I make a vow to Dezna here: I will tell her story, inject into it the same heart she put into my rearing. Her story is just one of many – of the typically nameless, faceless nannies who have raised a generation of American children, who are such an integral part of the infrastructure of our values, who have sacrificed so much.

"Yes, Miss Dezna, we are here," Maxine says, just behind me. "We are here, Miss Dezna." Her tone is haunting, as if she has a direct line to the chthonic realm.

Jellicia is tending to the fire and hangs the fish in foil over the flames for a crisp outer layer and tender inside. The cousins in attendance are enjoying the kick-down and start to sing. We eat the Jamaican Easter delicacy of Miss Birdie bun and cheese. Junior's daughter Ashanti sneaks up behind me and runs her hand through my hair and giggles as she runs away. Maxine and May are reminiscing about the old days, the ska parties and the dandy shandy, the hours spent listening to *Dulcimina*, the plates of gizzada and Jamaican black cake.

I am the only American here and the only white person for miles and miles. But I'm being hugged continuously and am cheersing over Red Stripes and dancing and holding hands and absorbing and laughing with these people who have become my family. I do not, for an instant, feel like an outsider. Perhaps I'd been experiencing all this kumbaya togetherness in slow-drip doses in my interactions with Dezna's family, but the importance of this day and my extended stay with them had made clear this familiar cohesion.

After all, for this occasion, I'd come to Jamaica for a week to stay in Maxine's house. I'd slept in a bunkbed; Cory, taking Dymar's regular bottom bunk, slept below me. This week was my first true immersion with the entire family.

ANOTHER MOTHER

At Dezna's gravesite, I think back to two days earlier.

***

I'm buckled in with Jelli and Blue-Blue in a van zipping down the road from Montego Bay to catch the sunset in Negril at the northwest horn of Jamaica, where the horizon is said to be awash in the mango hues of a rum cocktail.

Years without Dezna, and I still am reviving her through her family, through each countenance and the musical labba-labba of conversation.

All of a sudden on this drive, I realise I am Uncle Ross to Blue-Blue, this middle school boy in Jamaica who loves "maths" and proudly tells me he's a prefect for his underclassmen in the exact manner I would tell Dezna I had aced a spelling test. I hang on Dymar's every word as he provides narrated commentary of the scenery through the window – the Hip Strip or the vegetable market (he says, "vejah-tayble," like Dezna). He makes sure I know the exact moment we cross from St James into Hanover.

As we drive – here in Montego Bay, where Dezna had laid foundations, where she loved Cornelius, had sewn elaborate blouses before by some strange serendipity she ended up in Princeton – the tree line begins to darken on the horizon. We're not going to make it to Negril before nightfall. So we stop at a Tortuga storefront location to buy some rum cake and eat ice cream.

We cut our losses and turn to Maxine's house, the one covered with a cathedral of flaxen palm fronds, for a feast – the interior glowing from candles like a séance. Food is everywhere – salt fish, bammy, plantains, breadfruit, jerk chicken, curry goat, snapper drowned in coconut milk. There is, of course, mannish water, the Jamaican stew of a goat head, watery broth, bananas, yam, and spices.

Mannish water is closely associated with the nine-nights, also known as "dead yard" – the Caribbean's answer to sitting *shiva*, with a festive twist spanning longer than a week. Tradition holds that on the ninth night, the spirit of the deceased bids its valedictions as it passes through the party and gathers food. In this opportunity to mourn and celebrate with my Jamaican siblings, I realise we have formed a special bond. Maxine brings out photos Dezna had saved of my sister and me over the years. She even had some blown up to eight-by-twelve size. She also gifts me a key ring attached to a wood carving of Jamaica. One side says "Ross" and the other "Irie", which she tells me is the Dread-talk term for "peaceful" and "positive".

The next day, Easter Sunday, I wake up early as I'm inclined. Around the house, Maxine is up and about in the kitchen. She's cooking doughy dumpling. I give her a side hug and pick up yesterday's copy of the *Gleaner* newspaper to read from aloud. It's just the two of us before the world comes to life. We're chatting about the troublesome cat Marbles who is slinking around the backyard, and I put on some more water to boil tea.

"Tomorrow's the day," Max says wistfully.

"It will be a nice tribute," I say.

Just then, Max gets a call on her cell. I can hear Jelli's voice popping through the phone and Max's sped-up patois response is unintelligible to me. Max hangs up and sighs. She tells me a motorcyclist clipped Jelli's car at a nearby intersection, and she has to go fetch her.

Then she hands me the flipper, as the oil in the dumpling pan spits in plip-plops.

"You turn the dumpling when they're ready," she says, and I receive the kitchen utensil with gravitas.

When the dumplings are done, I place them on a paper towel-covered ceramic plate and put in the doughy ones Max had already pinched into the pan. Soon, May and Orville enter the kitchen to see this kid from New Jersey making dumpling in the family's Montego Bay outpost.

"What are you...?" May says, about to burst into laughter.

"Just making dumpling," I say as if this is only natural.

"And no saltfish fritters?" Orville says with a wink.

Once Jelli gets back and recovers from the annoyance of her accident, May, Jelli, and I head downtown for some shopping. The two head to a shop to look at weaves, and I enter but linger towards the front.

"I have no expertise in these matters," I say when May asks which of two options I prefer.

As we go to meet up with Orville to pick up the headstone, a man calls out to May, mistaking her for Fabi. And while we walk down towards Sam Sharpe Square, it seems every single person around the age of twenty knows Jelli.

"This is my Auntie May and Uncle Ross," she tells them.

I realise my role in Jamaica, whether fraternal or avuncular, is now crucial to my identity.

And now when I'm going down to Jamaica, and Dezna's children catch wind of the fact, I'm incorporated into their favourite past-time: asking if the traveller will be a courier for some gift or precious piece of cargo that needs to be delivered to a specific person. I know I'm officially accepted when they call me up and stick me with a few items – Magic Markers for Jelli's school or a small metal motor part for Dragon. "Hear you're going to the Rock," Orville or Maxine will say. And I make room in my suitcase.

***

Today, this Easter Monday, we huddle together by Dezna's grave for a feast of johnnycake, fried fish, dumpling, and jerk chicken. We're eating on greasy paper plates and taking refills of the kick-down. It is here, I realise, that I'm able to find what I've been looking for. In a sense, I didn't even quite know what I was searching for in trying to trace Dezna's steps, follow her journey.

After all, in my quest to track down some ultimate spiritual resonance in Jamaica with Dezna, I have searched high and low to attain a sort of enlightenment. As part of my journey to locate the truths of Miss Dezna, I was after some sort of oneness with her and with Jamaica. I wanted to attain a visceral connection to the island. As part of that pursuit, I once hiked Blue Mountain Peak, the highest point in Jamaica. I wanted to challenge myself physically and mentally to unwind after my weighty contemplations and somehow, in pushing myself to Jamaica's highest point, gain perspective.

ANOTHER MOTHER

Rydell, a dreadlock Rasta, shows up at the Alhambra Inn in Kingston on a Saturday morning to take me away to Whitfield Hall, a hostel and coffee plantation in an eighteenth-century building by the trail to Blue Mountain Peak.

I am to start my trek to the top in the middle of the night in order to arrive by sunrise.

In anticipation, I fill up with curry goat and sludgy coffee, hit the sack in bare-minimum quarters.

At Whitfield, a guide named Paul wakes me at two-thirty in the morning to begin our ascent. He's a young guy my age from the mountains and wears a Mickey Mouse sweatshirt and Nike sneaks.

I look up at the heavens. The stars appear stitched to the night sky. Eucalyptus trees stretch towards them, smelling like the Vicks Dezna often rubbed on my chest. On a clear day at the summit, they say you can see all the way to Cuba.

Half an hour in by the winding Jacob's Ladder part of the trail, I peer down to base camp where, ever so faintly, the kerosene lanterns glow.

With each step as I go to the top of Jamaica, I carry Dezna with me, imprinted as she is on my character. She motivates each trudge, my quads pumping up the mountain here in the dark. There is a certain *Are You My Mother?* sensibility to my upbringing in how I regarded Dezna. In connecting with Jamaica and its nature, I'm trying to find a spiritual connection. In going off-grid on this crazy hike in the dark, I reflect on her near amniotic influence.

Paul and I reach the summit where it is forty degrees before sunrise. Bless whatever force holds up those glorious Blue Mountains. We take shelter in a derelict structure where tourists used to spend the night. Out of torpor in the chill, we fall asleep so as not to feel the biting wind. I've become anesthetized to the pain in the mountaintop dreamland before bolting awake. Next, I watch the stars brush away like chalk into dawn. Paul rouses himself, and we observe the sun crack like a yolk through the clouds. Today it would be impossible to see Cuba, and we start our descent.

The familiar terrain we cling to strays from us in life – inevitably, like continental drift. Every year, the Tropic of Cancer moves almost half an arcsecond of latitude south, and the Tropic of Capricorn moves north at the same rate. The sunlight we feel upon our faces has taken so long to reach us. Light-years. During heavy years. And we launch ourselves ever onward into the future. That forward motion yoinks that dear past from us. And still we go searching for it. We grasp at nostalgia. We chase horizons.

For Dezna's children, grandchildren, and me, fate confiscated from us a future with Dezna far too soon. But her family and I have found kinship. Even though she's gone, our relationship has been given a second life in this newly formed family. It is in this bond that I've found my spiritual Promised Land, a personal Zion.

The breeze rustles here in Pisgah, up in the hills of St Elizabeth amid the agapanthus flowers, the peeny-wallies, the pineapple groves, and the breadfruit trees. The sardine tins littering the ground give the soil a metallic sheen. I close my eyes and listen to it, a silent meditation filled with the warmth of sunlight here. I am speaking in the voice of these hills, the same language, my other mother's tongue. My accent is inflected with the subtle St Elizabeth clangour of the terrain in the same way the rest of the family's accents are – maybe not fully, but subtly, years of seepage have bled through and left an inalterable glow. I have quite a mouth on me, people tell me. My voice glistens with the vibrations of these hills, and with each bombastic syllable, I find myself closer to my dear nanny, who was, and it is indeed much more accurate to call her as such, a mom to me.

I hum the old song that is at the forefront of my mind.

> Carry mi ackee go a Linstead Market
> Not a quattie wut sell
> Carry mi ackee go a Linstead Market
> Not a quattie wut sell

It is now time for the village men to start the complex operation of cutting into the grave stone tiles in order to lay the headstone. It is time, on this Easter Monday, to commemorate Dezna officially and lay her to rest – and, in some sense, resurrect her through a shared and consecrated bond with her family as a continuation of her legacy.

18. Redemption Psalm

The men are inspecting the situation. Dragon wants to cut an even square – two blue tiles over on Bready's side, two pink tiles on Dezna's, then two tiles up and two tiles down.

"Dragon, di tru hofishal ya, eem ago kut stone inna wan faam ar di hada," Junior says.

Dragon takes an electric saw and plugs in into an extension cord.

"Miss Dezna haf huh harijins and huh fyinal resting place," Junior says, narrating the scene and adding bonus commentary, as Dragon begins to cut the stone.

But when the saw blows a fuse, the men of Pisgah burst into a flurry of Jumiekan, patois so fast and loud I feel it in my chest. There's a debate between Wallace, a Rasta with a weathered, leathered face, and Dragon about the proper course of action to follow, whether they should try to get another saw or use a chisel.

"Mi fall sohwe inna di migl a di spekchrom," Junior says. "Bredda Wallace, eem need some edicayshan, di lego biis. Man krebe-krebe."

ANOTHER MOTHER

"Gwaan nuh!" Dragon says to Wallace as he shoos him away.

"Lowe me," Wallace shouts. "Lowe me!"

The saw is useless now. Sparks have flown, and the saw is still smoking from the blown fuse. Wallace is shouting more, trying to backseat-drive the process. Dragon decides to abandon the saw and busts out a chisel and a heavy rock with which to strike it.

Of course, things continue to get unruly. The men working on laying the grave stone argue about the correct methodology of removing the tiles and pouring concrete. All those Red Stripes and the kick-down now don't seem like such a good idea. Will the chisel offer a clear break along the sixteen tiles that need to be removed, or will the impact create fissures in the others? Dragon works enough construction to be confident in his chisel method. May, holding Diamond's hand, once again employs the vocabulary she's picked up in the West Palm Beach old-folks home and dismisses the arguing men.

"Oy vey," she says. "They're verkakte."

Wallace is getting heated.

"Yuh teck people fi cunnuh munnuh," Wallace says. "Zeen?"

"Puppageezus – man a bad man enuh!" Dragon counters. "Mi nuh ramp wid eediat. Why eem loud up di ting?"

"Dragon, eem a idden chrezha," Junior says to me. "Eem know wha fi do. Eem haf di hansa."

"Oono waan fi laan?" Dragon says tauntingly at the others as he instructs them in the proper way to use a chisel.

Maxine is suddenly talking about Edney. She continues talking to Orville about this person. Edney? I feel like I need to know who this is. I feel way out of the loop. *Who are they discussing?* I wonder. I'm embarrassed at not knowing. I finally ask, and Maxine indicates Dragon. Dragon? I've only known his Yard name. His real name is Edney, which sounds like the delightfully nerdy name of the kid who ruins the curve in AP chemistry class.

But just when things seem to be going smoothly, I hear all this yelling.

"Di raas?!" Wallace says.

"Wah di raas?" says another village onlooker.

It actually sounds like someone is calling my name. I keep looking over as the singular syllable of my name seemingly gets littered through fast streams of patois. By instinct, I keep looking up when I hear the sound – giving myself a case of ping-pong neck.

"Are they talking about me?" I ask Orville.

He breaks down in laughter.

"Di raas," he explains, is just about the worst thing you can say in Jamaican patois. It's basically, "What the fuck?" – with a harsher association attached.

"Raatid," Maxine says, in disgust.

The situation escalates – and quickly. Wallace and Dragon disagree about the proper way to pour the concrete.

"Di raas?!" Wallace says again, and I still turn by instinct. Wallace is challenging Dragon to a fight.

Orville and Dexter step in like bodyguards, and things calm down. Someone is wetting the cement with water in a foil mixing tray as Dragon removes the last few stray pieces of tile he's chiselled. Some of the village men take brooms and sweep the debris from the tiled grave and then take wet cloths and sponges to clean the rubble and plaster dust.

Into the open space Dragon has created, two men insert an inclined wooden base to be covered with cement on which the headstone will rest. Two more men pour the cement with pancake-batter bubbles onto the wood and cover the area Dragon chiselled. Placing the headstone on an incline on top of the wet cement, Dragon then takes a joint knife to smooth over any unevenness. Several of the village men place heavy rocks on top of the headstone so that it will set.

Nearby, I see Jelli break down. She cries an intense cry. Perhaps mercifully, the day has largely been without raw emotion given the practicalities of this honorific celebration. It was all about getting there, preparing the food, managing the logistics of the headstone. The flare-ups of the village men provided comic relief to the sadness, somehow without ruining the sanctity of the occasion. Orville, tough Orville, also takes some time to remove himself from the crowd and have a good cry by a guango tree. The legends of Dezna are legion in these hills. She treated many generations of people. The babies she brought from the brink of death and the elderly whose lives she extended – the hills sing in tribute to Miss Dezna.

Hafftanoon, Miss Dezna...Good heevlin, Miss Dezna. Here at the pink-tiled grave now affixed with a headstone, I am able to move past the weak Dezna in the hospital and find her in the pulse of her island. Her family all together – an additional child continuing on her legacy in the world and sharing in the camaraderie – helps her live on. Here we have the commingling of our spirits, a fitting catharsis to this journey.

The day, of course, is an exercise in imperfection. I stand with Maxine, May, and Diamond by the headstone as it's set before we pile back into the car. When we step away, Diamond brushes the wet cement with her shoe ever so slightly, the impression of the sole ridge of her sneakers kissed into the concrete corner. Then, Blue-Blue, walking across the wet tiles, falls hard. Cory catches the moment on video and, a few minutes later, shows the clip to Ivy.

Mother and son crack up good naturedly at the sliding belly flop. Blue-Blue looks up at them quizzically.

"It's from when mi fall on the stone...," he says.

The cadence of the afternoon lacks the sweet timbre of simple resolution. But it feels right, just having most of us together, a demonstration of our future family ties.

In finding Dezna's voice and my own, I've happened upon a new spiritual dialect. I recognise Dezna's ability to abracadabra misery into joy. In her received pronunciation, even something "soulless" managed to become "solace". By locating in the peach-pit of my throat that register in my voice, the letter finds the spirit. How I miss those Avalon days with Dezna in Princeton. The memories flicker in my mind like heat lightning:

Good, better, best

And I... will always love you...One and twenty, two and twenty, three and four and five and six and twenty...

Blue-Blue tugs at my shirt and asks if I want to see inside the house.

ANOTHER MOTHER

I'm hesitant and utter the elongated schwa of uncertainty.

"Come on," he says, throwing down his hand.

He creaks open the door which takes a tug to open, so seldom is it used, and we wander inside where old cooking pans and utensils sit in the kitchen. Tarpaulins cover furniture, and Jenga-configurations of cardboard boxes cordon off entire rooms. The house smells of mildew, and the sunlight shining through the windows illuminates the dust fluttering through the musty rooms. Cobwebs like the cotton Dezna and I used to stuff in pillows are strung in corners. We walk farther into the house towards its inner sanctum.

"This was Grandma Dezna's room," Blue-Blue says.

This is the bedroom Dezna shared with Bready. We look out through the window at the pineapple groves, the breadfruit trees with plump offerings weighing down branches. The family is migrating from the grave site on the left to the right side of the house.

We all move towards the veranda, Miss Dezna's knotty cedar veranda, looking out at the pineapple groves and the breadfruit trees as we share stories of our mother. The sky darkens a little in the distance. Birds chirp orisons at the horizon. We look out to where the world curves or drops off – I've never been far enough out to know for sure.

We gather on cedar chairs, or lean against the splintery banister. It's story time, now, and there's a certain reverence in the air, the kind Maas Seamon used to insist upon. We tell tales, the tales of Miss Dezna, as a fire burns below on the incline. Someone hands me a mug of bush tea, and I listen.

Acknowledgements

Blessings and gratitude to Ian Randle for receiving this out-of-the-blue book submission with such enthusiasm and giving the narrative a home at Ian Randle Publishers. Infinite thanks to Christine Randle for stewarding *Another Mother* through the publication process with masterful edits, keen attention to detail, and a sense of humor.

I am grateful to Larry Weissman, my agent, for championing my writing and coaching me through this book from its infancy as a proposal to a fully formed memoir.

It would have been impossible to bring this book to fruition without the love, support, and guidance of Dezna's family. I am eternally grateful to her children, Winston, Orville, Dexter, Maxine, May, Roddy, Carla, and Fabi, and her sons- and daughters-in-law, Ivy, Camille, Coco, Desmond, Vinnie, and Troy. I am honoured to be considered a brother. Dezna's grandchildren, Jellicia, Mikail, Junior, AJ, Ronique, Cory, Blue-Blue, Ethan, Diamond, and Joel, have all deepened my understanding of this beautiful family, its legacy, and its future. I am honoured to be considered an uncle. Lloyd, Dezna's brother, provided such texture to this narrative as I pursued it. And Rohena, Dezna's sister, and her husband, Frank, lent invaluable insight into Dezna's life in Jamaica and the United States.

Special contacts from my travels to Jamaica have become fonts of knowledge and support. I am grateful to Ainsley Cohen Henriques, Anna Ruth Henriques, Rachel Frankel (and the wider CVE family), and Marina Delfos. I extend thanks to the congregants at Shaare Shalom in Kingston and the Jamaican people on the island and in the diaspora who have been so warm to me during my many journeys.

Portions of this book previously appeared in somewhat altered form in certain publications. Chapters 1 and 3 use sections from "What My Nanny Left Me" in *Tablet*, Chapters 1 and 16 borrow from "When Parents Remarry (Each Other)" in *The New York Times*, and Chapter 5 excerpts from "Jamaica's Forgotten Jewish Pirates" in *Travel + Leisure*. Thank you to those outlets for granting me permission to use those passages. I am particularly grateful to Wayne Hoffman for fielding and handling with such care my initial essay at *Tablet* that became the germ for this book.

Dear friends Nadia Ahmad, Shane Allen, Tessa Borbridge, Jeff Burleson, Jane Elias, Seth Engel, Ania Jakubek, Nelson Wang, and E. Randall Younger all went above and beyond in offering detailed feedback on my manuscript. I appreciate your intelligence and generosity.

Encouragement and guidance from Will Barrett, Maud Bodoukian Meyrant, Willem Boning, the Borelli family,

Acknowledgements

Bianca Bosker, Joseph de Leon, Gabriella Fuller, Rose Hartman, the Lellouche-Giorico family, Adam Leverone, Lauren Lyons Cole, Eli Obus, HJ Pierce, Sarah Solomon, Jonathan Sweemer, Samara Terrill, Kit Tollerson, Vladimir Volkov, Jenny Xie, Eugene Yi, and Matt Zolan gave me an essential boost during my creation of this book.

My parents, Cindy and Irv, provided so much love throughout my upbringing. Though this narrative focuses on Dezna's strengths and influences, I am indebted to you for your many lessons and your support.

Nicole, my sister, has proven to be such a godsend throughout my life. I am thankful for her constant availability as a sounding board and source of wisdom. Thank you to my brother-in-law, Jordan, for your friendship and support of this book. In addition, I am grateful to my nephew, Dylan, and niece, Sienna.

To my wife, Tiffan: I do not for an instant take for granted your unwavering love, support, creativity, ingenuity, and no-nonsense edits. I am forever proud to count you as my co-conspirator and soulmate.

To Dezna: I am forever in your debt for everything I have conveyed in this tome and more. This humble tribute could never repay in full what you have given me. I hope to continue to do you proud. Love and One Love always.